Lachlan Philpott

THE TROUBLE WITH HARRY

OBERON BOOKS
LONDON

WWW.OBERONBOOKS.COM

First published in 2014 by Oberon Books Ltd
521 Caledonian Road, London N7 9RH
Tel: +44 (0) 20 7607 3637 / Fax: +44 (0) 20 7607 3629
e-mail: info@oberonbooks.com
www.oberonbooks.com

A catalogue record for this book is available from the British Library.

PB ISBN: 978-1-78319-082-9
E ISBN: 978-1-78319-581-7

Cover photography by Sarah Walker

Visit www.oberonbooks.com to read more about all our books and to buy them. You will also find features, author interviews and news of any author events, and you can sign up for e-newsletters so that you're always first to hear about our new releases.

This play is inspired by interpretations of the life of Eugenia Falleni. Falleni lived much of her life as Harry Crawford. Falleni was convicted of the murder of "her wife" Annie Birkett in Sydney in 1920.

'Falleni's story provides an opportunity to consider the depiction and treatment of one working-class, Italian-Australian man-woman in the 1920s…Falleni's wives were depicted as innocent victims, thus maintaining a heterosexual narrative. The refusal to conceive the possibility that Falleni's wives may have known him to be a woman and desired her as a man-woman was 'not a failure to know, but a refusal to know' and speaks of the threat of both lesbian desire and cross-gender identification, and of their power to disrupt heterosexuality and the male/female gender binary.'

Ruth Ford, '"The Man-Woman Murderer": Sex Fraud, Sexual Inversion and the Unmentionable "Article" in 1920s Australia' *Gender & History*, Vol.12 No.1 April 2000, pp. 158–196.

'When in middle age, she finally established an intimate connection, she was forced by her social circumstances and the strict moral confines of her day to maintain her deep secret from almost everyone, including her beloved.'

Mark Tedeschi Eugenia p 13.

'There is evidence to support almost any interpretation.'

Rebecca Edmunds, Researcher, Sydney Living Museums as quoted in *The Sydney Morning Herald*'s article He Was a She. But a killer? Feb 19, 2012.

The play has been developed with the support of The Australia Council, Belvoir, Brisbane Powerhouse, Cre8ion, Focus Theatre, The Playwrights' Center Minneapolis, The Playwrights Foundation San Francisco, TheatreofplucK Belfast, PlayWriting Australia and MKA: Theatre of New Writing.

I am indebted to Alice Livingstone and Pete Nettell for their original commissioning of this play, to Mark Adnum for his research support, to Niall Rea of TheatreofplucK Belfast for programming the premiere of the play and to Jane FitzGerald for her dramaturgy of the early drafts of this work.

Thanks to my long-term collaborator and mate Alyson Campbell who has played many pivotal roles in contributing to the development of this play.

This play was first produced by Theatreofpluck at The Mac Belfast as part of Outburst Festival in November 2013.

Harry Crawford	Michelle Wiggins
Annie Birkett	Louise Mathews
Harry Birkett	Matthew Mitchell
Josephine Falleni	Roisin Gallagher
Man	Gordon Mahon
Woman	Stephanie Weyman
Director	Alyson Campbell
Designer	Niall Rea
Sound Designers	Felipe Hickmann, Eduardo Patricio
Stage Manager	Siobhán Barbour
Costume Designer	Susan Scott

For their creative contribution to the development of this play I gratefully acknowledge the actors and creatives who include John Kachoyan, Julia Billington, Kate Box, Belinda Bromilow, Jeremy Cohen, Tahli Cohrin, Jeanette Cronin, Michael Cutrupi, Rebecca Edmunds, Sopa Enari, Teresa Famularo, Elaine Ferguson, Anni Finsterer, Jane FitzGerald, Robert Frost, Sam Haft, Josh Hecht, Damon Herriman, Celia Ireland, Gisele Joly, Jodie Kennedy, Alice Livingstone, Annette Madden, Sean Marshall, Rebecca Massey, Louise Mathews, Chris Mead, Matthew Mitchell, Andrea Moor, Amy Mueller, Shannon Murphy, Pete Nettell, Emma Palmer, Meredith Pennman, Cole Scott-Curwood, Will Sheehan, Nadia Tass, Jess Tovey, John Turnbull, Laura Turner, John Waters and Doris Yunane.

The Trouble with Harry – Introduction
Alyson Campbell

Lachlan Philpott's *The Trouble with Harry* deals with an interwoven set of ideas about sexuality, gender, race and class at the height of Victorian imperialism. Based on the true story of an Italian immigrant, Eugenia Falleni, who 'passed' very successfully as a man, Harry Crawford, in colonial Sydney from 1898 to 1920, this beautifully complex play wrestles with a largely hidden history and biography we might now frame, however problematically, as 'queer'. In this regard, the play adds to a body of artistic work and historiography that grapples with the problems of biography when the subject is not the dominant figure of modern history: the white, middle- or upper-class, heterosexual man. As an illiterate, working-class, not-white-enough (according to the White Australia immigration policies of the time) woman, Falleni could not author her own biography, so this output is based on archival research, speculation and, in the case of artistic works, poetic imagination. This speculation is rife because Falleni/Crawford was a 'female husband': she married two women, Annie Birkett and Lizzie Allison. The marriages were discovered in 1920 when a charred body that had been found in 1917 was finally identified as that of Annie Birkett. Falleni/Crawford was subsequently arrested and charged with her murder. There is a great deal of excellent research about the case, for example, Ruth Ford's essay '"The Man-Woman Murderer": Sex Fraud, Sexual Inversion and the Unmentionable "Article" in 1920s Australia' (2000), that is readily available and provides a more nuanced historical account than I will give here. Instead, I will try to offer some insight into Lachlan's process in approaching the material and what the play might contribute to the contemporary moment in Australian culture.

Lachlan is a brilliant writer of female characters, as is evident not only from the success of his plays *Silent Disco* (2011), *Truckstop* (2012) and *M.Rock* (2014), but also from his earlier plays *Catapult* (2002) and *Colder* (2008), where women, particularly older women, are evoked with depth, warmth and perspicacity. While Lachlan writes across a broad spectrum of topics, he is driven by a queer sensibility that particularly taps in to the urge to stage and give voice to the marginalised and disenfranchised. In *Bison* (2000/2009), *Catapult* and *Colder* this has been the Lesbian, Gay, Bisexual, Trans, Queer and Intersex (LGBTQI) community, *Catapult* and *Colder*, interestingly, putting a particular focus on the relationship between mothers and gay sons. Lachlan is interested in families and parenting: *Catapult*, for instance, merges gay and lesbian parenting with an existing mother/son relationship, creating a potent juxtaposition where each circumstance illuminates the other. His methodology involves gnawing away at a subject until he finds an oblique angle that pierces the familiar and renders it newly visible. This is no less the case in *The Trouble with Harry*, which at its heart is also concerned with family, sexuality and parenting, additionally informed this time by the lens of historical distance and the ethical dilemmas of biographical work.

Initially when Lachlan gave me the first version of the script in 2010, and I began working on the play and researching Falleni/Crawford, I had visions of staging lesbian subjectivity. The naivety of this assumption, and my own 'lesbian revisionism' very quickly became apparent: this is not a 'lesbian' story – the working-class women at the centre of it would not have been able to identify themselves as such at that historical moment. While the nascent field of sexology was identifying, or creating, taxonomies of sexual and gender identities, Falleni/Crawford and Annie, unlike Radclyffe Hall's Stephen in *The Well of Loneliness*, couldn't just pop into Daddy's library to raid the bookshelves and read up on their own condition (Hall, 2005 [1928]). What emerges, then, from contemporary sexuality studies and from the archival materials on Falleni is a huge question mark about the validity of making a piece of theatre about her that posits her relationship with Annie in any way as proto-lesbian.

Indeed, the research suggests that the fields of female masculinity and transgender expression may be more productive in relation to representing Falleni's experience and subjectivity. Philpott had initially begun the process of working on this play from that angle, interviewing trans people in New Zealand and Australia, with a particular focus on the idea of 'passing'. This focus is apparent in a research project carried out for the production, 'Passing through Transsexuality', where author Mark Adnum problematises the term 'passing' in relation to trans experience (2010: 5-9). He cites the Transsexual Road Map website (2010) as arguing: 'Passing implies a binary of pass or fail. It also implies a deception, as if you're passing yourself off as something you are not' (in Adnum, 2010: 9). Yet trans, too, is an identity that, at the turn of the twentieth century, was not available to a person such as Falleni, navigating a way through the undocumented, secret world of being a female husband.

So these issues of sexuality and gender identity remain deeply hidden, raising all sorts of ethical questions for a playwright attempting to make a work about this historical figure.

In light of this, the story of Eugenia Falleni/Harry Crawford is part of an Australian colonial history that can be told in many ways. The 'passing woman' is often 'normalised' through discourses that would have her passing for economic or idealistic reasons; driven to give up womanly comforts by the wholesome urge to fight for her country, or to join the ranks of 'Aussie battlers' as a 'colonial girl' taming a new land that was apparently up for grabs. What this 'normalising' does, in effect, is to resist the idea that women might want to live together in a loving and sexual relationship: it denies the possibility of sex between women. Renowned Sydney QC Mark Tedeschi, for example, argues vehemently that Falleni suffered from what would now be termed gender identity disorder, and was so 'firmly ensconced in his identity as a male that he viewed … brief liaisons with women as the product of a perfectly natural attraction felt by a male for a female' (2012: 46). In other words, there was no homosexual tendency in Falleni/Crawford. Tedeschi maintains that Eugenia/Harry kept her/his female identity hidden from Annie throughout their marriage. This interpretation continues to the present day in the media, legal and judicial narrative of Falleni's court case at the time, one that simply refused to conceive of a reciprocal loving and sexual relationship between (these) two women.

The Victorian moment marked an apex of interest in classification and taxonomy, from plants and animals to various qualities – gender, sex, race – of humans. Another layer of classification to consider here is the legal and media construction of Falleni as abnormal (and, therefore, criminal). As a Southern European immigrant she sits outside the hegemony of white Anglo-Australian culture and its immigration policies for a 'White Australia'. Under the Immigration Restriction Act 1901 'non-white' immigration was severely restricted. In principle this was designed to privilege Europeans, but in practice this meant British and Northern Europeans. Southern Europeans were largely excluded, so Falleni would fall into an unwelcome, outsider category, not only judged an outsider in terms of sexual and gender inversion but also race. The change in name from 'Falleni' to the Anglo 'Crawford' can be seen as another source of 'deceit' in these terms: as Falleni assumes the garb and role of a man, she also assumes the position of white Australian nation builder. As Philpott makes clear in the playscript, the Italian community in Sydney knows that she is a woman. On the other hand, Annie Birkett – constructed in these discourses not just as the 'victim' of sexual deception but the *white* victim – is portrayed in the play as denying knowledge of both Falleni and anyone outside the realms of white hegemonic respectability. When, in the play, a policeman comes to advise of the death of the old woman who has cared for Falleni's daughter, Josephine, and is looking for 'a Falleni', Birkett protests:

ANNIE: What sort of name is Falleni?
MAN: I believe it is Italian.
ANNIE: *Italian*. I see. I certainly know no Italians. We're a
     decent neighbourhood. Is there anything further?

Decency and the vested importance of the neighbourhood are values inherently connected to whiteness. Annie, lying/ pretending or genuinely duped(?), epitomises the urge to fit in, to belong, to cover up the unacceptable masquerade. In the play this is emphasised by her overwhelming concern for propriety, evident in repeated urges to 'be decent'. Her tenuous position in society is maintained only by her desperate efforts to fit into normative sexual, gender and racial requirements of the new white nation.

Lachlan does not want to 'normalise' Falleni/Crawford; instead he accepts that we cannot know how life might have played out behind their door and that this ambiguity is to be embraced, rather than coming to some clear conclusion and imposing that as 'the' narrative. This perspective has led him to the very challenging task of interrogating and developing a (queer) dramaturgy that does not pin things down or provide answers and neat endings. One begins to perceive the origins of Philpott's title: the unavoidable reference to Hitchcock's film, certainly, but also to Judith Butler's seminal feminist/queer text *Gender Trouble*. Lachlan is not interested in providing a single version of this story but in troubling easy assumptions that there is a single story to tell.

This has created the need to find dramaturgical forms that retain ambiguity. This, of course, is hugely difficult as in the theatre we tend to believe what we see; the combination of the embodied nature of performance and the prevalence of realist drama can tend to blur the distinction between character and performer for the audience. Lachlan has sought, therefore, to engage strategies that disrupt this relationship and the assumption that what we see is somehow the 'real' story (and, likewise, it is the director's job to build on these strategies in the performance dramaturgy). The most obvious device he has adopted here is the use of a chorus of Man and Woman – interlopers from the present who voyeuristically guide the audience through an exploration of the distant world of Falleni/Crawford and Annie Birkett. Functioning much as Genet's alarm clock in *The Maids*, that jolts the two maids out of their nightly ritual of playing Madame and, equally, jolts the audience out of the security of 'character', the Man and Woman undermine any security the spectator might feel. As an audience member, just when you start to feel there is something to cling on to the chorus will cast doubt on the reliability of the narrative or destabilise the moment, asking repeatedly: 'is that how it is?' Another dramaturgical decision Lachlan has made is to make Falleni's daughter, Josephine, the driving force in the play. This has the strange impact of decentering the material from Falleni/Crawford, heightening the sense that we get only the barest glimmer of direct access to the eponymous character. But this glimmer is powerful and moving. On shifting ground and framed by uncertainty, the rare moments when Crawford is encountered alone offer the chance of a felt, erotic connection with this figure from the past.

When I wrote the introduction to Lachlan's play *Bison* (2010) I noted the oddness of seeing his work go into print. Not because of the merit of the work – which is obvious – but because Lachlan rewrites prodigiously. *Harry* has proved possibly the most difficult play to settle on, largely because of this desire to avoid pinning down answers or losing the ambiguity. One change from the premiere production in Belfast (2013) to the Australian premiere seems worth noting here. This is Lachlan's introduction of the motif of Crawford's love for growing tomatoes. It is a potent metaphor: the tomatoes suggest Italianness, part of Falleni's 'otherness', but also the recurrent reference to something red that permeates the world of the play. The tomatoes are right. They replace a device in all the earlier versions of Crawford tending beloved orchids. While it may seem very odd for me to write here about something that is now excised from the play, the orchids give an insight into how Lachlan's writing works on a symbolic level to offer a remarkable crystallisation of the 'queer' subject being constructed at that moment. The orchid picks up on how Victorian classification and taxonomy-creation in the 1860s to 1920s were utilised as crucial strategies in nation-building (connected to empire and colonisation) and concurrent constructions of masculinity and femininity. Thus, while plants, including orchids, were hunted down at great risk and expense across the globe, and then placed into groups, genuses and families – and, literally, into 'Order Beds' at that seat of colonial botanical power: The Royal Botanical Gardens at Kew, in London – sexologists were creating parallel taxonomies of human sexual 'inversion', degeneracy, perversion and normalcy. Susan Orlean's book *The Orchid Thief* (2000) (made into the film *Adaptation*) colourfully documents the utterly obsessive and competitive nature of orchid hunting in the mid–late 1800s. She notes that 'orchids have always been thought of as beautiful but strange. A wildflower guide in 1917 called them our "queer freaks"' (2000:51). The orchid, then, put into symbolic service in the play, subtly drew together many aspects of this crippling taxonomy, classification and othering to show the construction of women existing outside of the heteronormative matrix as, essentially, 'queer freaks'. A fascinating horticultural trope of orchids is their practice of pseudocopulation. Many orchids, though by no means all, use pseudocopulation, which means that they effectively 'pass' as something other than a plant/orchid to attract a pollinator to them in order to achieve fertilization. This can be through pheromones, or producing fragrant oil or through looking very similar to the object of desire of their pollinator. The process allows the orchid to ensure its pollen is disseminated while effectively offering no reward: they get fertilized for real by offering a fake 'sexual' encounter with no payoff for the pollinator (Mackrodt, 2012). According to Ford (2000:166–7), the case against Falleni was based on fraud and deception: like the orchid, she is 'passing' as something other than she 'is', and those pseudocopulating women must be punished at all costs. This metaphor in the play, then, alluded to the assumptions of binaries and heteronormativity: that one is simply 'passing' as something else, not a thing in oneself (indeed, existing as a subject entails fitting properly into one side of this fixed gender binary); that the sex is fake (fraudulent), not real/right – not reproductive ('rewardless') and not even classifiable.

The dramaturgical process is a painful one, however, and we can't have it both ways! We do not often get insight into the elements that have been cut, but they are as much a part of the process of arriving at the final (*sic*) version as that which remains.

The orchids are fabulous but the tomatoes are right. Bursting on the one hand with colour, smell, fecund seeds and images of female fertility and, on the other, with connotations of the flash of rotten fruit thrown at an unseemly 'man-woman' charged with murder, but tried, ultimately, for gender transgression and penetration of a man's world, they offer a powerful merging of the otherness of Falleni's sexuality, gender and ethnicity.

This idea that women – decent women – would not and could not be having sex together is thrown into disarray by the revelation that Falleni/Crawford made and used a home-made dildo: the 'article' as it was referred to in the trial and the media at the time. With this knowledge all attempts to write off this 'passing' as purely economic go out the window. Here was a biological woman who had sex with other women. Everything else is unclear: did these other women know they were having sex with a woman? Did they suffer some 'deception' – as the normalising version of history that does not allow the possibility of reciprocal love and desire between two women would have it? Philpott gives the dildo a force in performance through a remarkable monologue that Josephine utters:

> Burrowing. I found the thing in father's drawer. The snake the…smelt it, held it, it made me laugh. Father heard me giggle, caught me with it, his drawer open and me with my fingers squeezing the…thing, rolling the thing about in my hands.

> I held it between us and asked him, *is this thing yours*? Here, Philpott succinctly and powerfully reveals the ridicule and revulsion the sex-aid produces – *and* also conveys with the repetition of the word 'thing' the lack of knowledge about, or even name or language for, existing sexual practices.

Falleni's dildo is evidence of sexual activity and, further, of a woman performing in a sexually active way in bed, rather than the assumed passivity 'appropriate' to her gender. Above all else, the existence of the dildo indicates that Falleni penetrates the apparently 'normal' and white female and thus usurps the place of men, not just economically (which apparently was forgivable in a good cause) but sexually, physically and emotionally. The appearance of 'the article' creates a problem in the process of constructing and shoring up the new medical, media and legal discourses and classifications that aim to establish and maintain heteronormative paradigms.

There is much to be gained in the contemporary moment from a theatrical engagement with this historical material. The experience of a non-normative subjectivity such as Falleni/Crawford in the emerging Australian nation brings sexuality and gender together with race and class in a way that is powerfully resonant in a contemporary Australia that is globally recognised as governmentally exploiting xenophobia and continuing to brutally marginalise indigenous peoples. In a moment dogged with continued misogyny and depressing homonormative gay assimilation into a strictly white, normative, economically self-sufficient mainstream, the play inherently sets up a powerful juxtaposition with a parallel historical moment and presents a chance for us to ponder our own assumptions about an inexorable 'progress'. For all the issues and complexities of staging an historical ('outmoded') femininity – the cross-dressing, passing, 'man-woman' we have largely lost – the play, and hopefully its many productions, have much to offer to contemporary discourses of normativity and to the range of (queer) performance we may have access to.

With thanks to Suzanne Patman and Hans-Wilhelm Mackrodt at Kew Gardens (where else?) for horticultural advice. Patman is now acting as horticultural advisor on tomatoes for the Australian premiere production...

References:

Adnum, M. (2010) 'Passing through Transsexuality', (unpublished). Research document prepared for Focus Theatre and Lachlan Philpott.

Butler, J. (1990) *Gender Trouble: Feminism and the Subversion of Identity*. London & New York: Routledge.

Campbell, A. (2010) 'Introduction', in Lachlan Philpott's *Bison and Colder*. Queensland: Playlab Press.

Ford, R. (2000) '"The Man-Woman Murderer": Sex Fraud, Sexual Inversion and the Unmentionable "Article" in 1920s Australia', *Gender and History*, 12, (1), pp. 158–196.

Freeman, E. (2010) *Time Binds: Queer Temporalities, Queer Histories*. Durham and London: Duke University Press.

Hall, R. (2005) *The Well of Loneliness*. London: Wordsworth Editions Limited.

Mackrodt, H-W, (2012) Interview with author, Kew Gardens.

Orlean, S. (2000) *The Orchid Thief*. London: Vintage Books.

Tedeschi, M. (2012) *Eugenia: A True Story of Adversity, Tragedy, Crime and Courage*. Australia: Simon & Schuster.

For Mark Adnum, His Excellency The King of Boodoo.

The Production was sponsored by Party Higher, Melbourne
The Trouble with Harry was supported by the Australian
Government through the Australia Council, its arts funding
and advisory body.

MKA: Theatre Of New Writing is supported by the Victorian
Government through Arts Victoria.

The Australian production was produced by MKA: Theatre
of New Writing with Darebin Arts Speakeasy and premiered
as part of Melbourne International Arts Festival on Saturday
October 18 2014 at Northcote Town Hall.

The cast:

Emma Palmer	*Woman*
Dion Mills	*Man*
Caroline Lee	*Annie Birkett*
Daniel Last	*Harry Birkett*
Maude Davey	*Harry Crawford*
Elizabeth Nabben	*Josephine Falleni*

Written by	Lachlan Philpott
Directed by	Alyson Campbell
Produced by	John Kachoyan
Set &	
Costume Designer	Eugyeene Teh
Lighting Designer	Rob Sowinski
Sound Designer	Chris Wenn
Production Manager	Amy Bagshaw
Associate Producers	Eric Gardiner and Corey Reynolds
Stage Manager	Harriet Gregory
Assistant Director	Alice Darling
Sound System Designer	Geoff Adams
Lighting Associate	Tom Warneke
Design Assistants	Rebecca Dunn (Costume) and Shane Thompson (Set)

Characters

HARRY CRAWFORD / EUGENIA FALLENI
early forties, to be played by anybody
but a biological male

ANNIE BIRKETT
mid thirties

HARRY BIRKETT
14

JOSEPHINE FALLENI
17

MAN
40 to 60, plays a range of roles

WOMAN
40 to 60, plays a range of roles

*This play is a fluid dance. Nothing is fixed in place,
nor should it be.*

*The space should offer a suggestion of both a domestic interior and the
surrounding street. The interior is Crawford and Annie's house, never
quite allowed to become a home. The exterior echoes the neighbouring
homes, streets, shops, pubs and the shadows of the laneways of inner-
city Sydney in 1917 to right now.*

*Man and Woman address us today and they inhabit both the same
and a very different space. Their identities should not be fixed either.
By this I mean they are not reporters, or neighbours or people who sat
in the court. They are man and woman and they can walk through
walls, freeze time, use microphones, cameras and other contemporary
tools of surveillance.*

Bird calls echo.

WOMAN: It's dawn at Lane Cove River Park/

MAN: A puppy circles a laughing/boy

WOMAN: /Boy throws a ball, pup chases, then catches a scent/

MAN: Some new smell in his snout/

WOMAN: Pup's nose in the air then to the ground/

MAN: He sniffs, whines, follows, stops.

WOMAN: There's something burnt black.

MAN: Puppy lifts his front paw, pulls back, yelps/

WOMAN: The boy's mouth drops.

> *Beat.*

MAN/WOMAN: Dead body.

MAN: Charred body.

WOMAN: Cooked remains of some poor wretch/

MAN: Some poor whore burnt black.

> *Beat.*

MAN/WOMAN: The crime site.

WOMAN: Police rope off blackened bushes.

MAN: Detectives arrive, stand huddled smoking next to the smoking bones.

WOMAN: Smell of burnt flesh hangs as a bat in a tree in the day.

MAN: Clues linger in the stillness after the struggle.

WOMAN: Forensic evidence, fingers curled.

MAN: Remains of skin grip splintered bone.

WOMAN: Well-worn shoes, broken teeth.

MAN: Frayed woollen cloth torn,

WOMAN: An empty bottle broken, cracked.

MAN: Some cheap chain ripped from a neck glints in the morning sun.

WOMAN: Veil of smoke blankets it all.

WOMAN/MAN: The burnt thing,

WOMAN: The detectives,

MAN: The lantana.

WOMAN/MAN: Kookaburra sitting in a gum tree looks the other way.

Bird calls end.

ANNIE enters in her best clothes.

WOMAN: That's her before the fray/

MAN: Before the feud/

WOMAN: Before the flickering flames.

HARRY emerges similarly dressed.

MAN: And there's the boy.

WOMAN: Look on his face – him knowing nothing.

CRAWFORD emerges.

MAN: And there *he* is./Before it all

WOMAN: Before it all. The rumours/

MAN: The revelations/

WOMAN: The headlines./Before:

MAN: /Before:

The family gets into position for a formal photograph.

WOMAN/MAN: The trouble with Harry.

A flash. The photograph taken, all disperse except CRAWFORD.

He remains alone and for a moment seems to sense the gaze.

He whistles a bright tune and takes a look up and down the street.

WOMAN enters.

WOMAN: This is the day they move to/Cathedral Street.

CRAWFORD: /Cathedral Street. Here we are then.

ANNIE enters. CRAWFORD smiles at her as they look about.

ANNIE: Help me with these boxes! They won't unload themselves.

MAN enters, watches them.

CRAWFORD goes and ANNIE takes a look along the street.

HARRY enters with a chest and trips over.

MAN: Boy drops the china and the mother lets loose/

ANNIE: My good plates!

HARRY shrinks away.

CRAWFORD: They'll be fine.

WOMAN: But it's him they notice. Something about him. A grin like butter wouldn't melt…

CRAWFORD winks at WOMAN.

A twinkle in his eye?

CRAWFORD whistles.

What a charmer.

He shakes MAN's hand.

CRAWFORD: I'm Harry Crawford.

MAN: And his handshake's firm./You know what they say.

WOMAN:/You know what they say.

CRAWFORD: And this is Annie. The wife.

ANNIE looks at them both then goes inside. WOMAN imitates ANNIE.

WOMAN: She thinks she's above it all?

MAN: Give her a/chance.

WOMAN: /Her name from the *first* marriage on the side of the tea chests./Birkett.

MAN:/Birkett.

WOMAN: A strange little bat of a thing. She draws the curtains and hides inside in the dark – never outside much longer than it takes to hang up smalls on the line, humming away hidden behind her knickers.

MAN: And then there's the boy.

HARRY returns and tries to whistle as WOMAN and MAN watch on. He can't manage it.

WOMAN: Left to fend for himself after/the stink.

MAN: /The stink.

HARRY looks about at his new yard.

WOMAN: It's near tea time. Sun going down, winter coming – air getting cold as mama's stare at an elbow on the table,

HARRY: Street lamps flicker/

WOMAN: Get the washing in!

HARRY: Tram bell rings/

WOMAN: Kerosene, burning wood/

HARRY: Garbage – piles of it burning/

MAN: And horse and dog and cat do – all of it always under your feet.

HARRY: A baby screams, a dog barks/

WOMAN: Bed bugs shit on stained sheets and run up and down the pillows,

MAN: Fleas jump floorboards. Rats rummage in the gutter.

WOMAN: Potato peelings in the sink, dirt under nails, grey meat dances as it boils in a pot.

A light on ANNIE in the kitchen. She hums.

WOMAN/ANNIE: I set the table.

ANNIE: Knives and forks/

WOMAN: Pepper and salt/

ANNIE: Cups and saucers/

WOMAN: Peas and beans/

MAN/WOMAN: Husbands and wives/

WOMAN: Love and hate.

MAN/WOMAN: The truth and the lies/

ANNIE: For a moment alone, just me.

WOMAN: But for the bugs and the mice and the fleas.

> *ANNIE sings.*

> The song she sings can be just hers.

> *The light above ANNIE lights up only her face.*

> Her song in the light.

> *ANNIE sings. MAN watches her sing in the light until ANNIE realises and shuts a curtain.*

WOMAN: Paint chips, seasons change and after a time they're not so new.

> *CRAWFORD whistles as he passes WOMAN.*

> Change the tune and keep it down! Enough to drive you to/

CRAWFORD: Just bringing some cheer.

WOMAN: That's what you call it?

> *HARRY crosses with a grocery box.*

HARRY: Old Mrs Bone's tongue clatters away like a tram –

WOMAN: Back inside young Harry Birkett, busy hands are happy hands, there's a lot of packing to be done.

HARRY: Yes Mrs Bone.

WOMAN: And every night at five o'clock the men/

CRAWFORD: The workers/

MAN: The husbands, the boys/

WOMAN: The larrikins, the chugalugs/

HARRY/CRAWFORD/MAN: All of us out none of us home.

HARRY: All in ties all of them grey/

MAN: Trudge from work to the pub/

WOMAN: Human steam trains – clouds of smoke sucked into their lungs and blown back out on the street to sit on a stool at the bar in the noisy pub.

MAN: Ten to six./Clock Ticks.

CRAWFORD: /Clock Ticks/

MAN: And every man in the bar

WOMAN: Every single rat on those floorboards shakes his sorry drunken neck,

MAN: Lines up empties cause it's closer to five to than ten to,

WOMAN: Time's henchlady shakes her fist,

CRAWFORD: She's coming to get us and pull us away/

MAN: From the fun to the cold hard dining table.

CRAWFORD: *(Jokes.)* The welcoming arms of the wife.

WOMAN: Potatoes boiling everywhere steam rising from saucepans to the fingers on the hands of the clock/

MAN: The bell gets rung – the bar hag shouts/

WOMAN: If you can't drink them leave them if you can't leave them drink them.

CRAWFORD: The coins all gone/

MAN: The drinks get skulled/

CRAWFORD: The doors get slammed/

MAN: And the pub gets shut/

WOMAN: /And the pub gets shut./They're out. He's coming.

ANNIE: /They're out. He's coming/

WOMAN: The bed bugs, the fleas,

ANNIE: The rats in the roof.

WOMAN: The mice and the moths, /they whisper –
he's coming.

ANNIE: /They whisper – he's coming.

WOMAN: Corned beef sweats,

ANNIE: Peas and chokos turn to mush

MAN: The women stand out on the street – pursed lips hands
on hips all/

WOMAN: Dinner's getting cold…

MAN: Kids whine, babies howl

WOMAN: Sausage spits fat from the heat of the stove, yells out
the window and all the way home to be decent/

ANNIE/MAN: /Show a bit of decency at least.

ALL: Be decent.

ANNIE sings again.

MAN: See her through the window.

WOMAN: The only one inside.

MAN: The only one not out for blood.

CRAWFORD enters.

ANNIE: There you are then. Cold out?

CRAWFORD: Getting so. What were you singing then?

ANNIE: Singing?

CRAWFORD: Heard you as I was coming up the street.

ANNIE: I was singing about love.

CRAWFORD: Love is patient love is kind.

ANNIE: Where's that from?

CRAWFORD shrugs. They kiss tenderly.

WOMAN: The eyes of the lady in the photo on the mantle stare out. Her mother, his mother, every grizzling old long-dead mother sighs and disapproves. If she could spit in his eye – lazy good for nothing lump of…

ANNIE pulls away.

CRAWFORD: What?

ANNIE: Nothing.

WOMAN: She would spit in disgust. If she could open her mouth and yell – but she is trapped in silence dead like she was trapped in silence living.

CRAWFORD notices a box on the floor.

CRAWFORD: What's in the box?

ANNIE: The boy brought it home. Guess.

CRAWFORD: A parlour game! A dozen bottles of good brown ale?

ANNIE: Wishful thinking!

CRAWFORD: A passion fruit cream sponge? A fresh ham?

ANNIE: Stop thinking of your stomach.

The box moves.

CRAWFORD: It's alive. Is it old Mrs Bone's head? Did he chop off her ugly mug? She still yelling/*you owe me for your rotten tobacco Mr Crawford.*

WOMAN: /You owe me for your rotten tobacco Mr Crawford.

They laugh. He tries to get at the box but she stops him. There is a sound from inside it.

ANNIE: Harry. It's a bantam.

CRAWFORD: A bantam! Open it up.

ANNIE: I don't like the look in its eye.

CRAWFORD: Go on! It won't be liking the dark. It might suffocate.

ANNIE: Won't, there's a hole in the side.

CRAWFORD: Annie.

He opens the box and looks at the bird.

Covered in lice. We won't be eating that tonight.

ANNIE: Harry! Don't say that. Upset the boy. He's afraid what you'll say.

CRAWFORD: Because he knows he's not allowed.

ANNIE: Harry?

CRAWFORD: What?

ANNIE: Let him. For a time?

CRAWFORD: He knows the rules.

ANNIE: But. Please?

CRAWFORD: Perhaps until we fatten it up a bit to eat.

ANNIE: Harry!

CRAWFORD: Sad-looking thing. It's a hen then?

ANNIE: Yes.

CRAWFORD: How do you know?

ANNIE:

CRAWFORD: How do you know? Look into its eyes.

ANNIE: No!

CRAWFORD: I think it's a cock.

ANNIE: Look into its eyes? How can you tell anything from/

CRAWFORD: Well that's about as good as looking through all the feathers for a thingamajig.

ANNIE: Harry! There *are* ways of finding out. Time will tell us without us needing to…

CRAWFORD: How long do we wait? No, I've changed my mind. He can't have it. We're not on a farm. You'll need to tell him.

ANNIE gives him a look.

You're the one who goes on about decency. Give him one of your talks about respectability. *What'll the neighbours say when they get woken up at the crack of dawn?*

ANNIE: It's a hen.

CRAWFORD: It is not a hen, look at the size of it.

ANNIE: They said it was a hen when they sold it to him.

CRAWFORD: Pulled the wool over the boy's eyes but not mine. How much did he pay to be tricked? It's a rooster and it'll cock-a-doodle-doo until they send us packing or we all go mad. It'll have to go.

ANNIE: He could train it to be quiet.

CRAWFORD: With a bit of wire around its beak? Cocks aren't dogs, love.

ANNIE: But – please give him a few days, Tally-ho?

CRAWFORD: Tally-ho Tally-ho. You know how to get what you want from me.

They look at each other. A smile spreads across ANNIE's face. She hugs him.

The morning it wakes me up I'll chop off its nut and we'll have roasted chook for tea. Speaking of tea…

He sits and rubs his hands together. She brings his dinner. He looks at the empty place at the table.

CRAWFORD: Where is our boy?

ANNIE: He's up the street.

CRAWFORD: Still working? Maybe he's buying a whole farm to bring home?

ANNIE: Harry… The boy was asking/

CRAWFORD: The boy was asking what? Can I bring home a bull?

ANNIE: No.

CRAWFORD: Not all that clap-trap about wicket keeping, he can't even catch.

ANNIE: No. He was asking how to shave his beard.

They look at each other. Something makes this moment awkward.

ANNIE finishes eating, clears the table, and goes out to her sewing. CRAWFORD affectionately watches her leave and remains at the table.

In the street, HARRY carries a box of groceries. He tries to whistle but can't get it. He stops and stares up at the sky.

WOMAN: That boy – like all the rest. Not much between his ears, not much meat on him either, all that running he does for penny pinching Mrs Bone. He'll probably get sent off to France, get stabbed dead in the mud.

HARRY feels the stare of mad MRS MURPHY.

Evening Harry.

HARRY: Evening Mrs Murphy.

She watches HARRY go.

WOMAN: If I could escape there, I would. I'd get away, let the French trench mud spatter my petticoat; find me a young soldier. Imagine the crisp uniform and me in a barn undressing him. Us hiding from the Hun in that barn, him and I, kissing first then…and after he's done it to me he falls asleep and I get into the uniform and I look like a soldier, leave him all white and bony on the hay, with a rifle in my hand and a purpose – an enemy to kill and I'm out of the barn and running – the krauts shoot at me, but I'm running fast, getting away from…

HARRY is home, tries to sneak past CRAWFORD. CRAWFORD gets up and blocks him and smiles. This appears to be a routine. They have a moment of fun trying to outwit each other but CRAWFORD wins out and HARRY concedes.

CRAWFORD: You've been busy.

HARRY: It was Mrs Bone.

CRAWFORD: Always is.

HARRY: Took such a time to get all the orders out. Then she asked me upstairs to help her.

CRAWFORD: I bet she did.

HARRY: Whenever I go up she has something she needs to show me or ask me and/

CRAWFORD: Did she give you anything extra for your troubles?

HARRY: No.

CRAWFORD: Nothing?

HARRY: No. But/

CRAWFORD: What?

HARRY: She played some music.

CRAWFORD: Music?

HARRY: Mozart.

CRAWFORD: That's something you can put in your pocket and save.

HARRY: It's not. No.

CRAWFORD: Something you can bring home and offer as a contribution isn't it? Pay for new arrivals?

HARRY: Oh.

CRAWFORD: Yes. Annie, the boy's home.

ANNIE: His tea's there/

CRAWFORD: Tell me this. How much did you pay for that mangy sack of lice?

What made you bring it home?

HARRY: It looked lonesome.

CRAWFORD: They told you it was a rooster?

HARRY: It's a hen.

CRAWFORD: What makes you think that?

HARRY: They told me.

CRAWFORD: And you believed them?

HARRY: Yes.

CRAWFORD: You believe everything you hear?

ANNIE enters, shows what she has been sewing – a coarse green dress. It's not very good sewing and they all know it.

HARRY: That looks like an army tent.

ANNIE: What do you mean?

HARRY: Put a red cross on it and all the sick soldiers can come inside you.

CRAWFORD: *(Jesting.)* Are you mocking your mother's sewing?

HARRY: Keep them safe from the Hun.

ANNIE: You are strange boy.

CRAWFORD: If I were you young Harry Birkett I'd be watching my tongue. Chicken little's life depends on it.

ANNIE: It's not finished but I need your help. I need to adjust it. I need one of you to put it on/

CRAWFORD: The boy will/

HARRY: I won't.

CRAWFORD: Well I can't.

HARRY: But I'm hungry.

ANNIE puts the dress on HARRY. He resists at first but then he gives in and enjoys it.

CRAWFORD/ANNIE: Oh, isn't that lovely?

ANNIE: Could have been my daughter!

HARRY: Very funny!

CRAWFORD and ANNIE laugh.

CRAWFORD: We're playing with you boy.

HARRY: I'm hungry!

ANNIE: Hold still then!

HARRY: Don't stab me with the pin.

ANNIE: I've got the shakes!

HARRY: Don't! You'll prick me.

CRAWFORD: Annie!

ANNIE/HARRY: Oooh!/Ouch! She got me!

ANNIE: An accident, wasn't deep.

CRAWFORD: Look on his face! She's kidding with you boy.

HARRY: But she/

CRAWFORD: Take a deep breath. Look at his face. What's that on your face?

CRAWFORD and ANNIE look closely at it and make a noise.

HARRY: What?

ANNIE/CRAWFORD: Fluff!

HARRY: It's not fluff.

CRAWFORD: You're covered in fluff, you'll be needing a razor.

ANNIE: My boy's becoming a man!

CRAWFORD: If he's going to shave do you think the boy might need some trousers?

ANNIE: Some trousers?

HARRY: Trousers! Would you?

ANNIE: Oh I don't know. I could try and sew some but… I'm very busy with all the mending. I don't know now, what do you think dear?

CRAWFORD: You do sew a lot already.

ANNIE: Mm. Women sew and men…men…

CRAWFORD/HARRY: Drink!

ANNIE: Yes. Men drink!

HARRY: Can I get trousers? Is it time?

ANNIE: If you stop whining like a girl and act like a man… We'll see.

CRAWFORD: Go and eat your dinner.

ANNIE: Don't sing at the table! If you sing at the table/

CRAWFORD/ANNIE: You won't get married for forty years.

HARRY: You two did!

CRAWFORD: You call that singing?

HARRY goes.

MAN: See them through the window in the rotting milky light.

WOMAN: A man and his wife, conversation in the night.

ANNIE: Does it look like a tent?

CRAWFORD: What do you want with another dress?

ANNIE: I thought we might…

CRAWFORD: What?

ANNIE: Go to the theatre or dancing. I thought/

CRAWFORD: You thought we might go dancing?

ANNIE: I just…

CRAWFORD: So you'll get dressed up to the nines and we'll be walking out the door and then you'll change your mind.

ANNIE: I don't plan it that way.

CRAWFORD: No.

ANNIE: We made it to The Tivoli that night.

CRAWFORD: We did./The Monster and the Girl.

ANNIE: /The Monster and the Girl. I was terrified of that monster/

CRAWFORD: Didn't even/look real.

ANNIE: /But you put your arm around me and I felt safe. You held me tight until they slaughtered him and I was so glad when he died. But the look the usher gave us.

CRAWFORD: He probably fancied you. If I'd have seen him I would've/

ANNIE: It wasn't that. He looked at us both, at us together… Something he saw…

CRAWFORD: What?

ANNIE: When we're out together sometimes people…look at us that/way.

CRAWFORD: /I don't know what you mean.

CRAWFORD and ANNIE sit in silence.

MAN: Lights going off up and down the street.

WOMAN: Bulbs snap to black in windows.

MAN: Things said like stars in a galaxy.

WOMAN: All the things left unsaid, the darkness between.

MAN: Up in number eleven Tommy Bracken gives Elizabeth Bracken a slapping.

WOMAN: In number nine Kevin Johnson picks at the hogget, gobbles it quick/

MAN: Before he gets caught – smacked on the wrist.

WOMAN: In number three the mother stares from the wall, accuses him of things she could never say out loud, reminds him to watch his back.

ANNIE gets up and closes the curtain.

MAN: Say your prayers, touch wood,

WOMAN: Bad luck awaits, peeks through door slits, ready to get you.

HARRY passes through for bed.

CRAWFORD: Harry?

HARRY: Yes.

CRAWFORD: Where's the bird?

HARRY: Out the back.

CRAWFORD: She better stay away from my garden.

ANNIE: Don't let her near his precious tomatoes!

CRAWFORD: Don't you start Annie! Did you clean your shoes for tomorrow, son?

HARRY: Yes.

CRAWFORD: Did you give your mother a kiss goodnight?

HARRY: Did you?

CRAWFORD: Yes.

HARRY: You didn't.

CRAWFORD: Not yet. Kiss your mother and tell her/

HARRY/CRAWFORD: Sweet dreams and sleep well.

CRAWFORD: I'm going to check that bird hasn't dug up my beauties.

He goes. ANNIE gives HARRY a little hug.

HARRY: Mrs Bone was asking me…

ANNIE: Mrs Bone was asking you what.

HARRY: What he does with all those tomatoes.

ANNIE: And what did you say?

HARRY: Said that while he waits for them to go red he tells them things he can't say to us.

ANNIE ruffles his hair.

Are you afraid?

ANNIE: What have I got to be afraid of?

HARRY: It's just that sometimes you seem... I don't know.

ANNIE: Your imagination gets the better of you. I'm not afraid of anything, love. Things are fine. They're good, aren't they?

HARRY: Yes.

ANNIE: Think of the kiddies at Frog Hollow. Poor little mites who don't even have shoes and dream of no more than picking a fat pocket at the football grounds. You're growing up so fast. You won't...

HARRY: What?

ANNIE: Cause trouble. Not you. You've always been so good.

HARRY: It's just...

ANNIE: Please, no questions about trousers.

HARRY: It's about... Father. Do you think he sees us from heaven?

ANNIE: I'm sure he does. Though how many of us he sees might depend on if there's a pub up there. Why are you thinking of *him*, boy?

HARRY: I don't know.

ANNIE: Then don't. Don't think about things long past dear. Say your prayers for what's to come.

He begins to do so. ANNIE watches him.

That's the way.

What are you praying for?

HARRY: If I tell you it won't come true.

You think he'll let me keep her? The hen?

ANNIE: He just might. He's got a good heart Harry.

HARRY: If she stays… I'd like to give her a name… I'd like to call her Lena.

ANNIE: Lena? Strange name to choose for a chicken. What made you think of that?

CRAWFORD interrupts them.

CRAWFORD: Cold out so I covered them up. We'll be needing the hot water bottles soon. And your feathered friend might freeze if there's frost.

HARRY: Can I bring her in?

CRAWFORD/ANNIE: No.

ANNIE: Get some sleep./Good boy.

CRAWFORD/HARRY: /Good night.

MAN: The husband and wife push the door shut,

WOMAN: Whisper in the dark.

MAN: As the boy sneaks that cock past their room.

WOMAN/MAN: Is that how it is?

WOMAN: She jumps under the covers as candlelight dances about on the walls.

MAN: Her toes twitch under the blankets as she giggles.

WOMAN: He gives her the eye, undoes his fly, the buckle of his belt clunks to the floor.

MAN: A little grunt, a sigh, then/

WOMAN: The squeak and strain of rusty springs.

WOMAN/MAN: That's how it is.

MAN: See the boy through the window of the little back room.

WOMAN: Holding that bird and looking out.

MAN: What's he whispering?

WOMAN: A prayer for something better in that stale room.

MAN: As lice from the bird hop up and down his arm.

WOMAN: A branch scrapes at the window and beckons the boy out.

MAN: The secrets hidden in the dark.

WOMAN: Things waiting to be held up under the light.

JOSEPHINE enters.

JOSEPHINE: When I was born I was given away. Father didn't want me and mother...mother.

Got passed on like some stray cat then the old woman took me. Now she lies upstairs, will die upstairs tonight. In the lightest room she will soon be dead and without her kind heart the world might go dark.

When she goes cold I'll pack my bag, go and find Father, knock on his door.

I stayed with him when the old woman hacked blood and they thought I shouldn't be near. That time she lived and I went back. But not tonight.

Tomorrow I'll have to track down Father at some new address. Cathedral Street. They moved again. They move all the time but every place is the same – the stink of the lanes and gossipy watch of the women. And in the house, Father wheezes through the night. The Birkett sews her way to salvation, stitch something coarse into something soft and hope nobody will notice the seam – cloth bunched like a prayer between her fingers.

I'll find their door and stand there. When they hear me knock they'll know. They'll open it up and see me, still young but something about me – my skeleton of secrets. Smile and all my teeth might drop like pebbles and clatter down their hall.

Morning. A rooster crows. CRAWFORD waits at the table.

HARRY goes to pass him to leave for school but is stopped.

CRAWFORD: You told us it was a hen.

HARRY: It is.

CRAWFORD: Then what was that racket this morning?

HARRY:

CRAWFORD: It's a rooster boy and you know what I said about being rid of it. It'll have to go or we will be evicted.

HARRY: No.

CRAWFORD: Go and get the bird.

HARRY: I have to go to school now.

CRAWFORD: You heard me boy. And bring the axe as well. I'm going to chop off his/

HARRY: No. Please. Don't chop off her head. She's not doing no harm. Please?

CRAWFORD: Oh, go on then. Go to school. We'll deal with your little friend tonight.

He goes. CRAWFORD goes as well.

WOMAN: Morning Crawford.

CRAWFORD: Mrs Snape.

WOMAN: Some ghastly crowing this morning woke Bubba up. You're keeping a rooster.

CRAWFORD: We won't be for long.

CRAWFORD winks and leaves.

JOSEPHINE enters, followed by MAN.

WOMAN: Who's that then?

JOSEPHINE scowls at her.

MAN: Looks like trouble.

WOMAN: Looks like/Crawford.

JOSEPHINE: /Crawford. Does he live here?

MAN: He does. And who might you be?

JOSEPHINE: His daughter.

WOMAN: Didn't know Mr Crawford had a daughter.

JOSEPHINE: Well there you go.

MAN: And what's your name dear?

JOSEPHINE: What does that matter to you?

WOMAN: We look out for each other, watch for thieves, lend a cup of milk if something's turned it sour. Your daddy lives in there.

JOSEPHINE at the door. ANNIE answers. They look at each other for a moment.

ANNIE: You found us.

JOSEPHINE: The old woman died.

ANNIE: Oh.

JOSEPHINE: I can't stay there now.

ANNIE: No.

JOSEPHINE: The undertakers took her.

ANNIE: That's what they do.

JOSEPHINE: Her eyes were open when she died and full of the fear but they pushed them shut. They put her in a box and took her up the hill to Edgecliff. Half way between...

ANNIE: What, girl?

JOSEPHINE: Home and the White City Fairground.

ANNIE: It won't be your home anymore. You better come inside then.

JOSEPHINE: Wonder if she could hear them screaming on the roller coaster.

ANNIE: Who?

JOSEPHINE: Her in her box.

ANNIE: We'll need to tell your father.

JOSEPHINE: Why? He doesn't care. Never came to see her. Never came to see me either.

ANNIE: I know that isn't true.

JOSEPHINE: I was sometimes visited by a *woman*.

ANNIE: Oh?

JOSEPHINE: And sometimes father sent things for me but... know him better through stories. The old woman told me so many. Good stories they were too with meat enough on their bones for a feed, but you probably know all the stories since you married him.

ANNIE: Don't believe every story you hear.

JOSEPHINE: I don't.

ANNIE: He did come to see you.

JOSEPHINE: I must have been out.

ANNIE: He's been busy enough making ends meet, getting money enough to pay for you to be there.

JOSEPHINE: Never asked to live with her. Father chose so father can...

ANNIE: What?

JOSEPHINE shrugs.

JOSEPHINE: So this is the new place. You and father move so often. I used to think it was because you were trying to lose me but then I figured it out.

Better than the last.

ANNIE: It's a decent enough street.

JOSEPHINE: Households are like little hotels.

ANNIE: What do you mean by that?

JOSEPHINE: People coming in and out and leaving all sorts of things so you know the lot.

ANNIE: There's a bed here for you as long as you need it.
I'm sure your father'll be…

JOSEPHINE: What?

ANNIE: Pleased. He'll be pleased to have you here.

JOSEPHINE laughs.

JOSEPHINE: And you? Are you pleased to have me here?

ANNIE: I'll do what's decent, girl.

JOSEPHINE: In your decent street. That's good of you. Where
is my father?

ANNIE: He's at work. And so is little Harry.

JOSEPHINE: Where does *father* work now?

ANNIE: At The Hero of Waterloo. He's a useful.

JOSEPHINE: I bet.

WOMAN looks through the window. JOSEPHINE sees her.

ANNIE: And now we have our own little hotel with beds to be
made and slept in then made up again.

JOSEPHINE: Who is that?

WOMAN turns away.

ANNIE: What are you talking about?

JOSEPHINE: Some woman looking through the window.
You didn't see her?

ANNIE: No.

JOSEPHINE: Might have been the hag I saw on the way here.
Stared at me like she knew everything passing through my
head, started asking questions about who I was.

ANNIE: Neighbours with nothing to do…

She shuts a curtain.

Best we mind our own business.

JOSEPHINE: Those eyes. Looked like poor old Mrs De Angelis. It might have been her ghost.

ANNIE: Don't say things like that.

JOSEPHINE: Well who else would she haunt now she's dead?

ANNIE: Josephine!

JOSEPHINE: If you don't like people staring you should take that ugly old crow off the wall. Don't know how you can bear her looking at you like that. Who is she anyway?

ANNIE: She's my mother.

JOSEPHINE: Scares the life out me.

ANNIE: Josephine!

JOSEPHINE: *Josephine, Josephine.* Why not make it easy and just call me Harry? Harry the son, Harry the daughter and Harry the/

ANNIE: It's not your name.

JOSEPHINE: How do you know? I could well be a Harry like the others.

ANNIE: What are you talking about?

JOSEPHINE: I could change my name. People do that.

ANNIE: You're upset. To lose somebody, even someone as old as Mrs De Angelis/

JOSEPHINE: You know, perhaps I am. I was looking through all her things. Things she collected because she thought they were precious. Treasures she hid from me and the other boarders. In the end they were easy to find. Such pathetic hiding places – so while she was lying nearly dead in the other room I was laying out all her jewels on the white bedspread, the one she was afraid to die on in case it stained.

Not much when you look up close. Things like that.

ANNIE: Perhaps you should…

JOSEPHINE: What?/Shut up?

ANNIE: /Have a lie down? Perhaps you should…

JOSEPHINE: Lie down? I'm not dying.

ANNIE: No.

JOSEPHINE: I don't need to rest. Do you think she's watching like your mother?

ANNIE: Who?

JOSEPHINE: Old Mrs D. She knew so many things about us. She knew *mother,* remembered much more than father about that sort of thing but then he is so useless at remembering. She told a good story. She would sit by me as I went to sleep, hunched like some old fish wrapped in a rug and tell me all sorts of things. She told all about father when he was…she told me about how you two met. The things she knew. Sad – all her stories gone to the grave and all that's left is stained petticoats and tin dressed up like silver. Rats picking through it all. That's why I left so quick.

Don't worry. I'm not going to stay here for long.

ANNIE: I didn't say anything about that.

JOSEPHINE: Didn't need to. When will the Harrys be home?

ANNIE: The Harrys?

JOSEPHINE: Imagine how funny it would be at a party.

ANNIE: At a party?

JOSEPHINE: Yes. *At a party.* You could say this is my son Harry and this is my second husband, Harry, second not third right? And this is Harriet, Harry's daughter but just call her Harry. I call them all that and it means I don't even have to open my eyes.

ANNIE: We don't often go to parties.

JOSEPHINE: No. I remember how dull things can be here. You with your sewing and him with his tomatoes. I might start doing jigsaws. To fit in.

ANNIE: Enough.

JOSEPHINE: What do you mean?

ANNIE: You know.

JOSEPHINE: No. I don't.

ANNIE: You think I've forgotten the last time you came and stayed? You think any of us have?

JOSEPHINE: How could anyone forget that terrible place, the wasps nest out the back and the in-bred neighbours smashing bottles all night. Is that why you moved?

ANNIE: I'm not talking about why we moved. I'm talking about what you did when you stayed.

JOSEPHINE: I…

ANNIE: Don't go digging around like that again.

JOSEPHINE:

ANNIE: Don't. You can stay here because of your father. You can stay here because you need to, since you probably drove the old woman to an early grave but you've got the devil inside you. I'm not inviting the devil to stay for long.

JOSEPHINE: The devil don't want to be here.

ANNIE: You'll need to find some work.

JOSEPHINE: I will.

ANNIE: There are jobs at the arsenic factory.

JOSEPHINE:

ANNIE: They'll be home soon. I need to get the tea ready.

ANNIE goes.

MAN: Look at her there staring up at nicotine-stained plaster vines on the ceiling.

WOMAN: Sour little thing. No wonder he's kept her at bay.

MAN: And what of the mother?

WOMAN: Died of fright in childbirth!

JOSEPHINE: Last time I stayed with *Dad* I had a little dig. Dig
in the dirt, through drawers, piles of things in the shed.
Things someone buried or hid, hoped would be forgotten.
Some wiggling worm's coming up to the surface. Dug
about and I found things. A tin. Not so well hidden – full
of feeble little secrets. I showed the boy, we went through
all the things inside. Things that didn't seem to belong to
anyone. The boy held them up, kept asking questions and
then we found the name on things... Lena. Lena...

Burrowing. I found the thing in father's drawer. The snake
the...smelt it, held it, it made me laugh. Father heard me
giggle, caught me with it, his drawer open and me with my
fingers squeezing the...thing, rolling the thing about in my
hands.

JOSEPHINE laughs.

I held it between us and asked him, *is this thing yours?*

ANNIE: *(Off.)* Come and help me with the potatoes, girl.
Josephine?

JOSEPHINE rolls her eyes and goes the other way.

MAN: The door slams. She runs up the street.

WOMAN: Up the hill down the hill, hear the sounds as they get
closer?

MAN: The sideshow on the wind?

WOMAN: The accordion playing songs for men who hide from
war.

MAN: Dirty children run in circles giggling.

WOMAN: Toffee apple grins, fairy floss fingers.

MAN: The rides and the freaks in the little alley at the side.

WOMAN: Twins born sisters but now bearded brothers.

MAN: The chicken man and his cock-cock-cocky old rooster
lady.

WOMAN: The girl who cut off her head with the butcher's knife, swapped it with her brother's, sewed them both back and then fooled mummy.

MAN: The boy who grew a tail and wagged it so hard it knocked the vase off the table, daffodils all over the floor.

MAN/WOMAN: And him.

JOSEPHINE: There he is.

MAN: Throwing darts at the balloons near the fat lady who shouts:

WOMAN: Danny Dart's never missed,

Come and see him throw,

Try and beat him without cheating,

Come and have a go.

MAN: And I see her/

He winks at JOSEPHINE.

JOSEPHINE: Danny sees me and he nods, I feel myself blush. Hello.

He always gives me a shot for free, stands behind me, holds my arms as I point the sharp dart and

JOSEPHINE/WOMAN: POP.

MAN: Darlin'.

JOSEPHINE/WOMAN: POP.

JOSEPHINE: He tells the fat thing:

MAN: I'm taking me tea break.

JOSEPHINE/WOMAN/MAN: POP.

WOMAN nods, picks at her fingernails with a dart as he leads her away.

JOSEPHINE: But Danny don't drink tea.

He drinks from a hip flask.

He takes me round the back where it's quiet, touches my
cheek and says/

MAN: It won't be long and I'll have money. We can leave this.
Be together.

JOSEPHINE: He kisses me, tongue all over mine. His hands
reach up my skirt and as the day melts away into night,
carnival music in my ears, I close my eyes and I see pretty
lights and laughing clowns as he has his way with me.
Lights all dancing and someone screaming in the distance.
Danny fucks me. Whispers in my ear – whispers/

MAN: Better get back to work.

JOSEPHINE: See you soon?

MAN: You bet my sweetheart.

ANNIE starts singing.

JOSEPHINE: I stand near the queue for the bearded lady and
watch Danny go back. Walk home thinking how it's going
to be, the two of us/

ANNIE: Where did you get to?

JOSEPHINE: I had a walk.

ANNIE: Fresh air's good for you. Nice flush in your cheeks.

Look at that. You've stained your dress. What is it?

JOSEPHINE shrugs.

I want to have a talk.

JOSEPHINE: Oh?

ANNIE: Things went wrong before didn't they Josephine?

JOSEPHINE: They did.

ANNIE: I didn't mean to…upset you. Since you'll be staying
here for a while…let's start again shall we? Your father'll
be home soon and the boy and… I'm sure it'll be nice. The
four of us. I know last time you stayed you were younger,

sillier. I can see you've grown up so I'm going to be decent and give you a chance.

JOSEPHINE sits down, hands in lap, and fiddles with a ring.

JOSEPHINE: I saw some soldiers on my walk.

ANNIE: I'm sure you did.

JOSEPHINE: Father didn't go to war.

ANNIE: No, he…where did you get that ring?

JOSEPHINE: From the old lady. She gave it to me before she died. Because I'd grown up so much.

ANNIE: It's lovely.

JOSEPHINE: Don't look too close.

ANNIE goes.

WOMAN: A man in a suit and a hat and tie coming down Cathedral St./Copper!

MAN: /Copper! It's the copper who came when the Murphys fought.

WOMAN: And the one who nicked Eddie Bracken.

MAN: Where's the copper heading?

WOMAN: Who's in trouble now?

MAN: Curtains gape open,

WOMAN: Heads pop over fences.

We hear ANNIE singing.

He's at number three! Crawford's door!

Knock at the door.

Bet it's the girl. Wonder what that girl's done?

Another knock.

JOSEPHINE: Birkett is oblivious; a toad singing at the sink.

JOSEPHINE opens the door and stares at the cop.

WOMAN: Neighbourhood spies dive to hide.

JOSEPHINE: Hello. What do you want?

MAN: Is your mother in?

JOSEPHINE: The singing hag out by the sink is not my mother. Who might you be, sir?

MAN: I've been sent by the courts. I'm looking for a Mrs Falleni. Is she in?

JOSEPHINE: Mrs Falleni?

MAN: Yes.

JOSEPHINE: The bullfrog's Birkett not Falleni.

MAN: And you are?

JOSEPHINE: Josephine.

MAN: Josephine who? Birkett?

JOSEPHINE shrugs. ANNIE enters.

Is there a Eugenia Falleni here?

ANNIE: Someone at the door?

Why didn't you say? Hello?

ANNIE pushes JOSEPHINE towards the kitchen.

Go and keep an eye on the stew girl.

JOSEPHINE pauses then goes.

How may I…

MAN: I'm looking for somebody. A Falleni. Eugenia, sometimes known as Lena Falleni. Do you know or have you ever heard of her?

ANNIE: Lena? My son has a chicken of that name. But I can't imagine you're/

MAN: She is in no trouble. I have some information concerning the death of a relative.

ANNIE: That's sad. But since I don't know her... What sort of name is Falleni?

MAN: I believe it is Italian.

ANNIE: *Italian.* I see. I certainly know no Italians. We're a decent neighbourhood.

Is there anything further?

MAN: No.

WOMAN: As the copper goes curtains snap shut in front rooms along the street.

Who's caused the trouble? Is one of the *ladies* in the house up to no good?

JOSEPHINE stands behind the WOMAN.

Who's done what behind whose back?

JOSEPHINE passes WOMAN and glares at her. Worried, ANNIE sits at the kitchen table.

* * * * *

MAN: The men are at The Tradesmen's Arms.

WOMAN: Yellow tiles to the shoulders./The stench of beer.

MAN: /The stench of beer.

WOMAN: They swill, they smoke, joke.

JOSEPHINE: I follow the copper to the pub.

/Copper goes inside.

WOMAN: /Copper comes inside –

JOSEPHINE: See him at the bar – jangling coins in his palm.

MAN: Thinking of finding Falleni, then thinking of ale.

JOSEPHINE: Father's in there, he's near.

CRAWFORD stands next to the cop.

He's just near that Cop; they're both at the bar.

CRAWFORD: /Evening.

MAN: /Evening. Getting cold out.

CRAWFORD: Freeze off your balls.

MAN: You're tellin' me.

CRAWFORD: You come here much? Not seen you here before.

MAN: Not from these parts – no.

WOMAN: What can I get you loverly gents?

CRAWFORD: New barmaid.

MAN: She's copping a few looks from the boys.

CRAWFORD: She's got more teeth than the publican's wife.

MAN: But does she bite?

WOMAN: Last drinks.

MAN/CRAWFORD: For the road?

MAN: Go on then.

JOSEPHINE: Father and the cop drinking inside.

Me at the window, the barmaid snarling/

WOMAN: What do you want here, girl? You know the rules. It's closing time. Clear off.

JOSEPHINE: I'm looking for my/

WOMAN: Everyone's looking for their daddy. He'll be out soon enough and if I were you I'd wait down the street away from what's about to hit you.

JOSEPHINE moves and waits on a wall.

ANNIE: It's back – the creeping feeling – something gnawing – dog at a bone, the feeling, starts again. Everything held together – bound together with anything we can find to keep it tight but it's all coming loose – getting ready to fall apart.

ANNIE packs a suitcase to leave.

JOSEPHINE: Men from the swill pour onto the street.

WOMAN: The copper, Tommy Bracken, Harry Crawford, full of piss.

MAN: *(To JOSEPHINE.)* Hello hello what have we got here then? A pretty young whore?

JOSEPHINE: Let me be, I'm waiting for my father.

As she says this CRAWFORD passes JOSEPHINE.

Father? Father/doesn't hear me. Doesn't see me in the dark leant on the peeling paint.

WOMAN: /Doesn't hear her. Doesn't see her in the dark leant on the peeling paint. /He just walks past.

MAN/JOSEPHINE: /He just walks past.

JOSEPHINE: He walks past and I don't know what to say and I don't know how to say it and I can't follow.

MAN: Street empty now.

WOMAN: And as if she's been drinking, that girl on the wall, as if she's just downed the beers and turned the glasses over on their heads – her muttering/

JOSEPHINE: Father/

WOMAN: But not moving/

JOSEPHINE: Father/

WOMAN: Whispering it at first, repeating it like all her marbles are lost and rumbling down the lane.

JOSEPHINE: Father?

WOMAN: Gets louder and harder then/

JOSEPHINE: Mother!

WOMAN: She drowns out the tram/

MAN: Stops the dog up the street who sniffs the bitch on heat/

WOMAN: Stops the mice and the fleas the rats the bugs.

MAN: Even Mrs Bone misses a beat – slips on the pedal as she plays herself a sad old song.

WOMAN: Some grey man pissing in the laneway stops – looks around/

MAN: That you Vera?

WOMAN: Piss dribbles on his fingers and shoes. But no mother comes.

MAN: Mother? She was shouting for her daddy.

WOMAN: That's not what I heard.

MAN: Clean your ears out love.

ANNIE's packing is frantic. She stops, stares at the picture of her mother on the wall.

It's dark in the street/

WOMAN: The corner shop's shut./Crawford's coming back.

MAN:/Crawford's coming back. Wonder what to?

WOMAN: Did that copper drop a bomb?

MAN: Who's been done and what did they do?

WOMAN: That rotten girl?

MAN: Birkett, the boy?

WOMAN: The whole damned lot of them?

MAN: The cops might lock them all away.

WOMAN: The eyes of the mother in the picture glare. Why they hung her up to smudge their lives in her face she will never know, but whatever's coming to them they deserve and she can't wait to see them get it.

CRAWFORD enters whistling.

ANNIE: There you are then. Is it cold out?

CRAWFORD: Getting so.

ANNIE: What were you whistling then? I could hear you coming up the street.

CRAWFORD: Did you think I was the dunny man with his big brown hands? Or the ice man with his blue ones. The paper boy? No! It was Tally-ho with a love song for his darling.

CRAWFORD tries to cuddle her and play about at a dance but ANNIE pushes him off.

ANNIE: You're drunk.

CRAWFORD: Not. Just had the one. What's wrong?

ANNIE: Josephine's come. The old woman's dead.

CRAWFORD sobers.

CRAWFORD: Dead?

ANNIE: Sad news.

CRAWFORD: Terrible. She was old but I did not expect…

ANNIE: The girl's in shock.

CRAWFORD: Shock?

ANNIE: Saying all sorts of nonsense.

CRAWFORD: Like?

ANNIE shakes her head; she doesn't want to talk about it. CRAWFORD touches her on the shoulder.

CRAWFORD: Harry will be pleased she's come. They always seem to have such fun. Remember that day at Billy Goat Swamp? The picnic. How they hid and we thought we'd/

ANNIE: What I remember's the trouble she caused.

CRAWFORD: There was that.

ANNIE: Another mouth to feed.

CRAWFORD: We'll manage.

JOSEPHINE enters, overhears.

She won't stay long. And she won't go snooping again. She learnt her lesson.

ANNIE: She's always at me.

CRAWFORD: What's she been saying this time?

JOSEPHINE comes into the room, stares at CRAWFORD. He doesn't get up.

JOSEPHINE: I went to find you but I wasn't sure where to look. I tried to get into the hotel but they pointed me to that back room.

CRAWFORD: The sow's hole.

ANNIE: A hotel's no place for a woman.

JOSEPHINE: Did she tell you?

ANNIE: Tea's ready.

JOSEPHINE: Did she tell you?

CRAWFORD: Yes and I'm sorry for your loss. Did she suffer?

JOSEPHINE: It was horrible. She screamed like an ogre from the pain and she wet herself with sweat and urine. She hacked up blood and…no. She died in silence.

ANNIE: Eat your tea.

JOSEPHINE: Not hungry. Whatever it is smells like death.

ANNIE: Death?

JOSEPHINE: Death everywhere all around me and what am I to do?

Pause.

CRAWFORD: You can stay here.

JOSEPHINE: Then what? I got no job.

CRAWFORD: You can find one. A girl like you.

JOSEPHINE: As somebody's maid? How long will that last?

ANNIE: Perhaps if you watched your tongue a bit.

CRAWFORD: Annie.

ANNIE: You've had a shock. Let's all have some peace. Eat up and be quiet.

They eat.

When you're done there you can get some rest. You'll sleep in the front room.

JOSEPHINE: I'd like to wait up for Harry.

CRAWFORD: He'll be late tonight. Old Mrs Bone sends him here and there in the dark of night. Treats him like her slave boy.

JOSEPHINE: But there's a storm coming.

CRAWFORD: He's a big boy.

ANNIE takes JOSEPHINE's plate.

ANNIE: Go and lie down dear. I'll bring some warm milk.

JOSEPHINE: But you'll tell? About…

ANNIE: Not now girl.

JOSEPHINE: Then when?

She goes. CRAWFORD sees the case.

MAN: And through the slit in the curtains I can make them out. Is he saying?

CRAWFORD: Packed your things again I see Annie.

ANNIE returns and faces CRAWFORD.

WOMAN: What's being said?

MAN: Something like this?

ANNIE: That girl is a plague she always brings trouble. The police came today. I'm not having the boy raised around this.

MAN: Or something like this?

ANNIE: They came looking for Falleni.

CRAWFORD: How would they…

ANNIE: Maybe the dead woman planned it all. Mix up some name in a letter to plant a seed of doubt so they investigate. All they need to do is knock on the door and every neighbour's tongue is wagging.

CRAWFORD: She wouldn't have…

ANNIE: Wouldn't she? Everybody watches us. Will we have to live like rats…hidden in the dark?

WOMAN: Or this?

MAN: Maybe it's like this?

CRAWFORD: Tell me about what?

ANNIE: It's nothing at all love. A copper came to the door looking for some foreigner.

CRAWFORD: A foreigner?

ANNIE: An Italian. Odd mistake – but the way people move about, guess they just had the wrong address. The neighbours must have thought we had ourselves a bit of trouble but the copper left soon enough. How's the stew?

CRAWFORD: Needs salt.

CRAWFORD stands behind ANNIE and puts his arm around her. They are silent.

MAN: The girl in the front room sits on the spare bed.

WOMAN: Wind outside blows secrets about – things tapping at windows.

MAN: Shadows dance on walls.

JOSEPHINE/WOMAN: Distant thunder comes closer.

JOSEPHINE: The blanket. Wool scratches my neck and arms.

The sound of rain, someone laughing up the street.

Feel hungry but I couldn't eat dinner. Think of the sideshow, the lights swinging in the wind and fizzing in the rain. Danny Dart.

The old woman's gone. The smell of her room – Bible next to the bed, John the Baptist's head on a platter.

Overheard the truth whispered once while I lay praying in the dark.

Now I know to close the door and not bother praying.

HARRY enters with milk.

HARRY: You awake?

Mother told me to bring this in.

JOSEPHINE: Thank you. You worked late.

HARRY: Yes.

JOSEPHINE: Why are your fingers crossed?

HARRY: Mrs Bone and I… We saw a white horse.

JOSEPHINE: So?

HARRY: If you see a white horse you have to keep your fingers crossed until you see a dog.

JOSEPHINE: Or what?

HARRY:

She wrestles with him and gets him to uncross his fingers.

JOSEPHINE: Now you'll find out.

HARRY: I'm sorry to hear the news about your grandmother.

JOSEPHINE: She wasn't my grandmother. I was taken to her by… *father* when I was very young. She used to tell me she was my grandmother.

HARRY: But she wasn't?

JOSEPHINE: What difference does it make? That's what she wanted to believe.

HARRY: Who was she?

JOSEPHINE: Some barren old woman who couldn't do better than stillborns. She told stories of how she kept trying and every time cords wrapped around their necks or…

HARRY: Why did you live with her?

JOSEPHINE: So father could work.

HARRY: What happened to your mother?

JOSEPHINE looks away.

JOSEPHINE: You learnt to whistle yet?

HARRY shakes his head.

Have things been good here? Since you moved?

HARRY: Mother sews and he smokes and mutters away at his tomatoes.

JOSEPHINE: All the secrets they must know.

HARRY: I have a chicken. A rooster.

JOSEPHINE: Which then?

HARRY: A rooster. Lena.

JOSEPHINE: Lena?

HARRY: *(Whispers.)* Because of the name on the tin we found. Those things in the tin in the shed. I thought…

JOSEPHINE: What? Finding that was our secret Harry. Don't you remember what I said? You don't think things through do you? What did my father say when he heard the bird's name?

HARRY: The only thing he says is if she keeps waking us up, he'll kill her.

JOSEPHINE: He couldn't kill a flea.

HARRY: Been trying to blindfold her so she thinks its dark and stays quiet.

JOSEPHINE laughs.

Sorry about the secret.

JOSEPHINE: Bit late now.

HARRY: Yes.

JOSEPHINE: Look at your face. Like the bearded lady.

HARRY: A bush ranger!

JOSEPHINE: All that fluff.

HARRY: Your father's going to teach me how to shave.

JOSEPHINE: I bet he is.

HARRY: It's Saturday tomorrow. No school!

JOSEPHINE: We can go and see the freak show. See the porcupine lady.

HARRY: The big fat man. Maybe we'll beat Danny Dart. /POP.

JOSEPHINE: /POP. Maybe not.

HARRY: But if we go we can't tell mother. She doesn't like the fairgrounds, the folk there frighten her. People like that.

JOSEPHINE: People like what?

HARRY: Mother'll make us go to the gardens. For the *fresh air*. She's going to make me trousers, Josephine what's a fuck?

JOSEPHINE: A fuck?

HARRY: Yes.

JOSEPHINE laughs.

JOSEPHINE: You don't know?

HARRY:

JOSEPHINE: I could tell you but I reckon you should ask your mother.

HARRY: Really?

JOSEPHINE: Yes.

HARRY: Thank you. I should let you rest. Goodnight.

JOSEPHINE: Goodnight.

HARRY goes.

MAN: The boy's light snaps shut.

WOMAN: And so does the girl's.

MAN: What do we know about the lady and lord of the manor?

WOMAN: About what do they do? The two of them?

MAN: Yes. What do they do in bed?

WOMAN: They lie under blankets in a candle-lit room – looking forever into each other's eyes, a joke, a story a/

MAN: No. He tells her it's time and turns out the light/

WOMAN: He reaches into the drawer for the…thing. /Ooh yes!

MAN: /Ooh yes!

WOMAN: He rolls it and slaps it between his hands.

MAN: He covers her mouth as he rips up her gown/

WOMAN: One hand over her eyes, the other clutching the end of it,

MAN: He parts her legs fumbles a bit and rams right up her/

WOMAN: No.

MAN: Yes.

WOMAN: No. He doesn't go into the bedroom at all.

MAN: Then what?

WOMAN: She knits, waits, sighs, gives up. Turns out the light.

MAN: Seeing all the lights are off, he creeps through the house, out the back door crosses the grass, goes into the shed.

CRAWFORD lights a candle.

WOMAN: He's reaching about behind the tools to find /
the little tin.

MAN: /The little tin. Butterflies on the lid.

WOMAN: Pale blue wings flutter on the rust.

MAN: Through the crack of the door of the shed.

WOMAN: The whistling man and his butterfly tin.

CRAWFORD opens the tin. He slowly goes through the items in the tin, looking at them carefully, placing them out.

Leave him some privacy.

MAN: Don't you want to see?

WOMAN smiles. She does.

WOMAN: A cufflink?

MAN: A photo of some man and a girl.

WOMAN: A little doll/

MAN: A yellow ribbon/

WOMAN: A hair brush/

CRAWFORD hums softly.

MAN: A handkerchief with an embroidered peach.

WOMAN: No whistling in there. Is he humming under his
breath?

MAN: In the stillness, yes. The things from the tin sitting there
next to the tools on the bench in the shed.

CRAWFORD: I'm sweeping and Mother calls me in.
My brothers and sisters surround her swarming, buzzing,
mutts needing more attention than they'll get – Mama
telling – yelling that since I am the oldest I will need to
learn about sacrifice, that she cannot do all this alone.
The look on her face because she knows, can see Father is
ill, that Father will die and when he does, she just sits there
glaring at his cold body laid out on the bed.

Father's pillow, faint smell of tobacco and sweat, reaching for his clothes in the wardrobe, his trousers round my legs, his cap over my ears and I go that night take flight while they all sleep.

One by one, he puts things back in the tin.

Run from being my mother's slave – free for the first time. That salty boat, the smell of paraffin, gulls circling, diving – all those men – none of them know – I'm one of them me and them and the drink and the jokes. I realise I am free. Free.

CRAWFORD thinks about the ship and then comes to.

WOMAN: Behind the tools.

MAN: Behind the door.

WOMAN: He hides the tin.

MAN: A quick trip to the dunny.

WOMAN: A quick wee and then into bed with her./Her.

MAN: /He sits on the seat. Door ajar pale yellow light and he's/

WOMAN: There's a drop of blood in the water and another and another/

MAN: He's humming something tuneless and then he's looking down between his legs.

WOMAN: A drop of blood in the water and another and another/

MAN: And he's sitting there /cursing

CRAWFORD: *(Muttered.)* Cursing this curse – flaming mutt of a friggin cunt.

HARRY enters.

WOMAN: Muttering – dabbing with little squares of newspapers/

MAN: He doesn't hear the footsteps pad on the grass.

WOMAN: Doesn't hear the cough; doesn't see the shadow in the pale spill of light.

MAN: And then/the boy is there.

CRAWFORD/WOMAN: /The boy is there.

CRAWFORD and HARRY face to face.

WOMAN: The boy and the blood in the pale yellow light.

MAN: The Harrys.

WOMAN: One looking up.

MAN: One looking down.

They are both frozen in the moment.

CRAWFORD: Harry?

The boy runs.

CRAWFORD: Harry?

A storm begins.

MAN: What has been said fits into a crack in the earth before the rain.

WOMAN: What hasn't been fills the sky above.

MAN: You can see it all when the lightning cracks.

Lightning cracks.

Saturday morning, sunshine after the storm. We hear LENA crow.

ANNIE unpacks her case. CRAWFORD passes her whistling and gives her a kiss. He heads out to the garden and picks snails from his tomatoes and drops them into a bucket of salt.

HARRY enters with LENA. He has slept outside and looks wet. He watches CRAWFORD for a time until CRAWFORD notices he's there.

CRAWFORD: Good morning Harry.

> *They can't bring themselves to make eye contact so they focus on the bird.*

CRAWFORD: She's a pretty chook isn't she? Something about her. Here's me saying we'll have to do away with her when…she's a part of the family now.

Your mother's excited about the picnic today. She's been looking for you. I think she wants to measure your legs. For trousers.

HARRY puts LENA down and goes.

Harry…

You will be good won't you? You won't…

ANNIE and JOSEPHINE set up a picnic around them. JOSEPHINE scratches her legs.

CRAWFORD: Stop scratching. What are you, a dog?

JOSEPHINE: It's the bed bugs.

ANNIE: Not in my house. Tell your daughter to mind her tongue.

CRAWFORD: Mind your tongue.

ANNIE: Things are so fresh after last night's rain. Like it washed everything away. And Daddy found snails on his tomatoes this morning. Tell them.

CRAWFORD: They were sliding up the stem.

ANNIE: Lucky we had the salt.

CRAWFORD: Not for them.

ANNIE: No.

CRAWFORD: A sprinkle's all they need and they foam up and die.

HARRY laughs.

JOSEPHINE: That's just plain mean.

HARRY: What's it matter?

CRAWFORD: He's right. What's it matter?

HARRY: There's animals with no point at all. Stupid animals that show God wasn't concentrating properly. There is no point in any of them living. They just annoy us.

JOSEPHINE: Is that what you think?

HARRY: Yes.

JOSEPHINE: Don't they teach you anything at school?

HARRY: Not about snails. And fleas and bugs and slaters. What is the reason for a slater? I'd kill them all. I'd take them from the dirt and muck and kill them like a fuck.

CRAWFORD: Harry!

ANNIE: What's got into you?

HARRY looks at CRAWFORD and exasperated gets up and walks away. CRAWFORD motions for JOSEPHINE to follow. She does.

ANNIE: Language like that and he'll never get trousers.

JOSEPHINE: Harry? Harry?

She catches him.

What are you doing? What's wrong?

This isn't like you Harry.

HARRY: Everything's going to fall apart again. Just like…

JOSEPHINE: What do you mean?

HARRY: I can't say.

JOSEPHINE: Can't say what?

HARRY: Do you know?

JOSEPHINE: Do I know what Harry?

Harry?

Tell me.

Tell me.

HARRY: Last night I woke up and went out. I didn't realise but your father was in there and I saw... I can't say what I saw. I can't even think of it – what I saw.

JOSEPHINE: What did you see?

HARRY: He was in there and...he bled. Blood on the floor. Blood on his hands and...

Is he sick? He's sick and he's going to die just like Father did and Mother will be sad again. And we will have to move and I...

WOMAN: What does she say to him? Does she say/

JOSEPHINE: Are you sure it was blood? He was probably fiddling about with his tomatoes.

MAN: Is it that? Is that what she says? Or does she say/

JOSEPHINE: You were probably half asleep and dreaming Harry. Some vision. Look, he's fine this morning. It'll be fine.

WOMAN: Or is it:

JOSEPHINE: I need to tell you something Harry.

HARRY: What?

MAN: There? She's going to tell him there?

WOMAN: There. Yeah. What do you care?

MAN: What's she going to tell him? What words will she use to say it?

CRAWFORD approaches them.

CRAWFORD: You two should come and have something to eat. And Harry?

HARRY: Yes?

CRAWFORD: Behave yourself and watch your tongue. For your mother's sake.

There is a moment of uneasiness between the three of them then we hear a pianola and drunken singing.

WOMAN: Saturday night. Cathedral St.

MAN: Pianolas wheeze, ale bottles clink.

WOMAN: Rat on a pipe watches through the window.

CRAWFORD: We should go out.

ANNIE: Out?

CRAWFORD: Dancing.

ANNIE: Where would we go dancing?

CRAWFORD: Somewhere with an orchestra and a chandelier. You could wear that new dress. I'll watch the eyes of every man in the room turn and see you when we walk in… would you like to do that?

ANNIE: I'd like to dance with you but…

CRAWFORD reaches out for her.

MAN: Is it like this? Between them? In there?

WOMAN: While the trams rattle past and they massacre songs up the road in the smoked-filled boarding house.

ANNIE pulls away.

CRAWFORD: What's the matter?

ANNIE: I thought somebody was watching.

CRAWFORD: Watching what?

She turns away to shut the curtains.

ANNIE: It feels queer.

CRAWFORD: Queer?

ANNIE: It's Josephine. She watches us. Sees all sorts of things…

CRAWFORD: Then I shall call out and wake her right now and tell her she should leave.

ANNIE: Don't be silly.

CRAWFORD: Then… What?

ANNIE: She knows.

MAN: The music next door stops.

WOMAN: A clock ticks on the wall/

MAN: A dog barks and the boy comes in,

HARRY: Goodnight.

CRAWFORD/ANNIE: Goodnight.

MAN: A hacking cough in the distance/

ANNIE: Don't let the bed bugs/

WOMAN: Then nothing but the clock again/

ANNIE: Bite/

CRAWFORD: Of course she knows. She knows everything.

ANNIE: But the boy…

CRAWFORD: He doesn't watch us like her.

ANNIE: With her here things get more complicated. She might tell him what she knows. And not just Harry.

CRAWFORD: Why would she do that?

ANNIE: That look she gets in her eyes. I see it. I just worry.

CRAWFORD: Don't worry now. Josephine's asleep. The whole world's asleep love.

ANNIE: Dreaming about how to get us no doubt.

CRAWFORD: What do you want us to do? Hide?

They stare at each other.

Annie? Do you remember that day at Clarke's?

ANNIE: The first day I saw you.

CRAWFORD: I'd seen you before that.

ANNIE: But we'd never…

CRAWFORD: No. When you first saw me, what did you think?

ANNIE: When I first saw you? Harry, I…

CRAWFORD: No, what did you think?

ANNIE: I thought you looked decent.

CRAWFORD: Decent?

ANNIE: Yes. I thought I'd be proud to walk through town with that man on my/arm.

CRAWFORD: /Arm in arm, right through the centre of the city. The two of us together.

CRAWFORD and ANNIE stare into the distance.

MAN: Is it like that?

WOMAN: Or more like the rest?

MAN: Tommy Bracken's back hand swinging after drink.

WOMAN: Moira Murphy sobbing for her son dead in a ditch in Dunkirk.

MAN: The silence of the Snapes as cigarettes burn down and newspapers yellow.

WOMAN: Broken bottles, chipped promises.

MAN: Just like every house on the street?

The light goes out.

JOSEPHINE checks the coast is clear and leaves the house.

CRAWFORD cannot sleep. He returns and drinks at the table.

CRAWFORD: That salty boat, gulls circle and dive and shit on everything – all those men – and their drink and smut/

JOSEPHINE: Slip out in the dark, go down to the freak show – the fairground the dancing lights the wind up sounds, know where he'll be. There he is. Danny! Danny? He drags on the last of a cigarette, throws the butt, points a dart. POP./ He don't see me.

CRAWFORD: /They don't see me. I hide it well until one night plain and bright as the stars in the sky – the captain sees. He pulls me aside asks me to report to his cabin. A little drink together and we talk and talk. A slip of the tongue and him locking the door as he says: *There's something I've noticed about you.*

JOSEPHINE: Then there's this woman this girl in a red dress big mouth like a dog and Danny's got his arms 'round her.

CRAWFORD: The cabin rocks and my lips pursed, my legs together, my arms by my side. His hands reach out – his hairy hands tugging at me as he whispers let's find out then Mr Crawford. Let's find out.

JOSEPHINE: His arms round her as if she's me. He whispers something to her and the look, the look he gives her and the way she smiles.

CRAWFORD: First hands on my buttons then ripping at my shirt, the smell of his sweat the whiskey on his breath – my arms by my side me saying no and his breath as he's saying: We'll see about that. We'll see.

JOSEPHINE: He takes her by the hand, nods to the fat woman who doesn't even stop shouting and Danny pulls her up the alley. I follow and stand in the shadows and hear it smell it./Trousers falling.

CRAWFORD: /Trousers falling. The ring of the brass belt knob as it hits the floor. His dirty fingers inside me, warm spit from his mouth in mine – close my eyes and I rock with the room. In the cabin in the night out at sea under all those stars./The price.

JOSEPHINE: /The price. No more shots for free now. I shrink into the dark.

JOSEPHINE returns.

CRAWFORD: You scared me half to death. Sneaking out all day and night. Where have you been?

JOSEPHINE: Nowhere.

CRAWFORD: You have.

JOSEPHINE: I've been up at the fairgrounds.

CRAWFORD: The freak show? We know that's where you go.

JOSEPHINE: So?

CRAWFORD: Nothing good'll come of going up there.

JOSEPHINE: You can say that again.

CRAWFORD: What are you doing up there girl?

JOSEPHINE: Nothing.

CRAWFORD: Then don't waste time going.

JOSEPHINE: I won't. If I want a freak show I can stay right here. Harry told me what he saw last night.

CRAWFORD: What on earth do you mean girl?

JOSEPHINE: Want me to say it out loud?

CRAWFORD: Say what?

JOSEPHINE shakes her head in disbelief.

JOSEPHINE: Do you think you can keep it a secret forever?

CRAWFORD: We all have secrets. There's no need to talk about them.

JOSEPHINE: But I need to talk about it. I need to/understand.

CRAWFORD: /Talking never helped. People do nothing but talk about things and look at where that gets them.

I did what I thought was best for you Josephine, you know that don't you?

Now do the same for me. Go to bed.

She goes. CRAWFORD remains at the table staring at the bottle.

* * * * * *

WOMAN: Early morning on Cathedral St. A young man in uniform. William Thompson!

MAN: Mrs Murphy.

WOMAN: Leaving today? /Going off to fight the war?

MAN: /Going off to fight the war.

WOMAN: I remember the day you were born Billy. Your father staggering home from the pub telling everyone he'd finally had a son. God be with you.

MAN: And with you.

WOMAN: The births and the coffins

The summer, the cold.

MAN: The dogs, the cats.

LENA crows.

WOMAN: That blasted bird.

CRAWFORD leaving for work passes them and nods and whistles as he leaves.

Mr Crawford.

HARRY enters petting LENA.

JOSEPHINE: Harry? I spoke to Father. About the… He's not dying. He's not sick. He said he's fine so…don't worry. Forget what you saw because it was silly.

JOSEPHINE looks suddenly unwell.

WOMAN: The girl turns white as milk, vomits all over the garden.

ANNIE: Lovely that is, all over your father's beauties/

MAN: She runs to the dunny for the second round – door slams, swings back and forth.

ANNIE: You alright in there Josephine? Josephine? Go to school boy. I'll handle this. Off you go.

He goes.

JOSEPHINE: Something I ate.

ANNIE: And what might have that been then? That you ate?

JOSEPHINE: The rissoles?

ANNIE: And not the first morning like this is it? I know the signs.

JOSEPHINE: Signs?

ANNIE: Yes. How long has it been?

JOSEPHINE: I don't know.

ANNIE: We better get you to a doctor then. To be sure.

JOSEPHINE: I'm fine.

ANNIE: Get yourself changed. If you can't be respectable at least you can look it.

WOMAN: Smell of antiseptic in the silent waiting room. Nothing being said.

MAN: Nothing needing to be said while the boy is at school, the father at work.

WOMAN: Nothing to begin a conversation with in this room with the curtains drawn, wick alight on dynamite burning down.

MAN: Come through, girl.

JOSEPHINE: Doctor's fingers prod and poke.

ANNIE: Hold still girl, let him have a look.

JOSEPHINE: His fat face blank and then/the news.

ANNIE: /The news. Doctor asks/

MAN: How old are you?

JOSEPHINE: Seventeen.

MAN: And the father?

MAN goes.

JOSEPHINE: Walk home and she's saying:

ANNIE: Last thing any of us need.

JOSEPHINE: Yes.

ANNIE: You do know that don't you?

JOSEPHINE: Yes.

ANNIE: If you're quick. If you're quick then you could deal with it.

JOSEPHINE: You mean?

ANNIE nods.

JOSEPHINE: Then Birkett rushes ahead – so when she gets to the top of our street she isn't too close to me.

WOMAN: Take a look! The girl who came to number three? Everything alright Annie Birkett? Crawford's girl's not looking so well.

ANNIE: Mind your own!

WOMAN: *(Whispers.)* Have you heard?

ANNIE: Josephine! Come inside!

WOMAN: Expecting a little one at number three.

ANNIE: You better get out and clean off the tomatoes.

WOMAN: You can bet we won't be seeing its daddy.

ANNIE: Shall I tell him or will you?

JOSEPHINE: I will.

ANNIE: So you've decided?

JOSEPHINE: Yes.

ANNIE: And?

JOSEPHINE: I want to keep it.

ANNIE: You want to keep it? Then you better tell him quick. He may ask you questions but I suspect/

JOSEPHINE: What?

ANNIE: That he won't want to know. Tell him though. Best you do. I won't keep your secret. Do you know who the father is?

JOSEPHINE: Yes. No.

ANNIE: Which?

JOSEPHINE: No.

ANNIE: So we'll be sending you to the nuns then?

JOSEPHINE: To the nuns?

ANNIE: How else do you expect to survive? You can't expect your…you cannot expect us to support you, not with a little one.

JOSEPHINE: I'll get a job.

ANNIE laughs hysterically.

ANNIE: A job doing what? You don't even know the father. No hope. Know what they call girls like you?

JOSEPHINE: No.

ANNIE: You'll find out.

JOSEPHINE: You must know this story. Isn't that what happened to you?

ANNIE: It certainly is not.

JOSEPHINE: Well it happened to father. I can be like him.

ANNIE: What did you just say?

JOSEPHINE: You heard. I'll be like father. Get rid of the kid – fob it off to some old woman and then I can meet myself some decent lady and we can make believe for the rest of our lives.

WOMAN: Eyes meet – blood floods faces.

JOSEPHINE: How dare you laugh at me when you're no better.

MAN: Water bubbles, hisses on the stove.

JOSEPHINE: How dare you call this nonsense when your whole life is pretend.

ANNIE: You think all of this is pretend?

JOSEPHINE: What? You think it's real?

JOSEPHINE laughs in ANNIE's face.

MAN: Birkett turns to the stove, picks up the saucepan/

WOMAN: And hurls it at that little vixen.

JOSEPHINE screams.

MAN: Wet walls/

WOMAN: Steam scalds/

MAN: Burns her arms/

WOMAN: Her hands/

MAN: Her legs/

WOMAN: Her face.

JOSEPHINE: How could you do that to me?

ANNIE: Wish I'd killed you. I want you to leave this house. I never want to hear from you again.

JOSEPHINE goes to the street.

WOMAN: See the girl in the street all wet and red and welting, kneeling, hands on her ears.

MAN: What's happened then what's wrong?

WOMAN: Where is your father dear?

MAN: Time stands still/

WOMAN: Lights wince/

MAN: Words sting/

WOMAN: Blisters bubble.

JOSEPHINE shakes her head, her posture becomes limp.

JOSEPHINE: My father?

WOMAN: Yes.

JOSEPHINE: I never knew him.

WOMAN: What dear?

JOSEPHINE: I never knew him. Not my father. You mean that thing walking around the street? He's not my father. He's my mother.

MAN: Everyone stops still on the street.

WOMAN: No curtain moves,

MAN: No dog barks,

WOMAN: No bug bites.

MAN: The door of number three doesn't open.

WOMAN: You heard what the girl said?

MAN: *He's my mother.* I heard.

WOMAN: Everyone crowds around the burnt girl.

MAN: Words she yelled whirr like music as questions dance about in the fading light.

WOMAN: Things repeated behind hands. We never gossip – never speak ill –

MAN: Never speak out about anybody/

WOMAN: Keep things quiet – mind our own business – but the news it spreads in a matter of minutes.

MAN: If that is the case, if the knocked-up girl's not mad/

WOMAN: She's not mad/

MAN: If he is a she pretending to be a he then what does that mean about her/

WOMAN: Who?

MAN: The wife? Does that mean she knows?

WOMAN: She must.

MAN: Then what does that make her?

WOMAN: If she knows then that makes her what?

MAN: And him?

WOMAN: Who?

MAN: Him?

WOMAN: Who? Her?

They laugh.

WOMAN: Nobody asks the girl in. No cold water, no cup of tea.

JOSEPHINE leaves.

She just disappears with the light of the day./And it's nearly six. Clock ticks.

MAN: /And it's nearly six – clock ticks.

CRAWFORD enters.

MAN/WOMAN: It's him!

MAN: He's coming!

WOMAN: Him?

She laughs hysterically. CRAWFORD stops suddenly as if he senses he's being watched. He sees nothing.

ANNIE sits in the front room in darkness. CRAWFORD enters and turns on the light.

They look at each other. The bulb breaks.

HARRY: Josephine's gone. They fight in hissed whispers. Can't hear what's being said, just her snarling and him snapping back when she does. On it goes through the night. No dinner and later when I sneak out to the dunny Mother sits at the kitchen table in the dark, only light the blue of the gas burner – he's nowhere to be seen.

LENA crows.

In the morning their door's shut, nobody about. No fire in the kitchen. It's cold and I just go to school. Out on the street I pass a soldier on a crutch. He's still in uniform but not wearing the smile he left with – his leg disappeared with the smile too but I don't know in which order – which one got blown away first. Me and the soldier just look at each other. Feels like somebody should sing something for him. But I don't have a song.

ANNIE surfaces, she looks tired, stares at the picture of her mother then cusses, turns away.

Finish school and I go to Bone's store, Virgin Mary scowls at me from the corner. Mrs Bone there with a cup of tea and a bun for me saying/

WOMAN: Something wrong with you today?

HARRY: No Mrs Bone.

WOMAN: No whistling?

HARRY: No.

WOMAN: Have people been saying things?

HARRY: What things?

WOMAN: Just a whole lot of gossipy claptrap nonsense rumours. So promise me this young Harry Birkett…if you hear them don't listen just block your ears and sing God Save the King.

HARRY: Yes Mrs Bone.

WOMAN: Or get your whistling right! Now, there's a box of things to take to Mrs Murphy and then… Harry?

HARRY: Yes?

WOMAN: How would you like some time away? I thought we could go to the seaside. Up to Collaroy? Get away for a bit?

HARRY: I'd like that.

WOMAN: I bet you would. Take the box then…

HARRY stands on the street with the box in the stillness.

MAN: A couple passes Harry...

HARRY: Morning Mr and Mrs Snape, how are you both doing/today?

MAN: /The couple looks away.

HARRY goes.

MAN: Just the two of them in the house now.

WOMAN: Echoes of it all, of/the day they came here.

MAN: /The day they came here – how quickly they moved in became just like everybody else.

WOMAN: Did they? Just like us?

MAN: That first day I met them I thought they were decent enough.

WOMAN: Her hidden away like a bat?

MAN: *Him* whispering sweet nothings to his tomatoes?

They laugh hysterically.

CRAWFORD: What'll we do now?

ANNIE: Will I leave you or will you leave me?

CRAWFORD: What do you mean by that?

ANNIE: Now the boy's away there is hardly any need to pretend. I won't run again. And we can't stay here.

CRAWFORD: We could try.

ANNIE: Try what?

CRAWFORD: To sort things out. Or we can move on.

ANNIE: Again?

ANNIE gets her suitcase out.

CRAWFORD: Annie please.

CRAWFORD attempts to touch ANNIE but she brushes him off.

ANNIE: You're in my way.

CRAWFORD: Shouldn't we give it one more try?

ANNIE: What's the point?

CRAWFORD: How about we get some fresh air. A picnic? Let things sort themselves out – out in the open.

ANNIE: If that's what you think/

CRAWFORD: Let's try and work things out.

MAN/WOMAN: That last day/

MAN: They leave the house together.

WOMAN: Grim-faced with a blanket and a hamper.

MAN: Clinking bottles in the basket.

WOMAN: He always liked the drink.

MAN: The look on their faces as they come out the door.

WOMAN: And steal up the street. Like…

MAN: Just like…

WOMAN: What? What are they like? Just like what?

MAN: Their arguments trailing them almost caught them up/

WOMAN: Their doubts just jumped onto the tram, they're with them on the track,

MAN: Truths chase them through the bush, hear the twigs snap and the bracken bend, flick back/

WOMAN: The lies hidden in pockets and in the picnic basket, peer through the wicker/

MAN: Their secrets giggle and poke fun – whisper how it must look at a distance when really it's like this/

WOMAN: They find a clearing just down from the flour mills.

ANNIE spreads a red tartan rug.

MAN: He gathers kindling, whistles grimly in the bushes.

WOMAN: He screws up the front cover from yesterday's *Truth*, fiddles with matches, curses as one after the next – black on his fingertips. Then finally/he fans the flames.

MAN: /He fans the flames. She opens the basket. Some bread and some ale.

WOMAN: He swigs, offers her none,

MAN: She snatches bread,

WOMAN: Tears it gobbles it down.

MAN: They're alone.

CRAWFORD: This is nice then isn't it?

ANNIE: Nice?

CRAWFORD: Yes.

ANNIE: You're behaving like an animal. Drinking straight from the bottle and pulling me about like a bag. What are we doing here anyway? It's way too late for this.

CRAWFORD: Behaving like an animal because that's how you've been making me feel – like a dog /when

ANNIE: /When what? What is it you want to say?

CRAWFORD:

ANNIE: For god's sake. You're the one who thought it might do us some good to get out of the house so we could clear the air. Why you dragged me all the way over here I'll never know, but we're here now so speak.

Silence. ANNIE laughs.

But it is the same as ever. You've got nothing to say. I thought it'd be different with us. Remember the stories I told you about the first? About how sad and lonely it was? When I met you I thought it would be different, I thought that we could…

CRAWFORD: What?

ANNIE: What does it matter now? I've been such a fool. Wasted so much time and your own devil of a daughter saw it all for what it is. Like some cheap trick in a sideshow. Everybody knows. Everybody sees you for what you are and if they don't laugh at you then they must think how sad you are, how sad I am because…

CRAWFORD: Don't. We've been doing fine. Right as rain.

ANNIE: You can't think that. Dressing like a man is one thing but thinking like one… We're doing fine?

They look at each other for some time.

ANNIE: I used to look at you and feel something. When I knew you were coming home, I'd sing. Now I sit in the dark and hope it'll swallow me up.

CRAWFORD: Why?

ANNIE: Why do you think?

CRAWFORD: We can move and start again. Make a fresh start?

ANNIE: We never had that.

CRAWFORD: What do you want to do?

ANNIE: I want to get away and I don't want you following. I'll take my boy away and we can start again. I have to be done with you.

CRAWFORD: What will I do?

ANNIE: You've always survived alone Harry Crawford.

CRAWFORD: I can't survive without/you.

ANNIE: /You'll find another if that's what you want. You can spot them. You found me.

They both sit drinking in silence. It gradually becomes dark.

MAN: The light is fading. The darkness grumbles deep below.

WOMAN: Along the river at the picnic grounds row boats get paddled to shore, blankets folded, crumbs left for birds.

MAN: There's no one else left.

ANNIE: You know what I think? Nobody made you become what you are.

CRAWFORD: That's what you think?

ANNIE: Yes. You chose.

CRAWFORD: I chose? You think that I chose this?

They look at each other for a very long time.

CRAWFORD gets whiskey from the basket and drinks from the bottle. ANNIE joins him drinking but CRAWFORD stands away from her, he looks out into the distance.

WOMAN: The fire flames crackle and rise.

MAN: The arguments and secrets and stories surround them in the glow.

WOMAN: Do they edge closer on that blanket to keep the secrets out?

MAN: Glare at the stories that twist in the dark?

WOMAN: Drain the things they know away in drink?

MAN: Do they smudge as one in some dark dance they can never have in light?

CRAWFORD and ANNIE dance the dance they could never have together.

WOMAN: In the darkness no one sees,

MAN: In the darkness no one knows.

WOMAN: He says he loves her but his voice is strained and hard.

MAN: He reaches towards her, she pushes him.

WOMAN: He falls,

MAN: She runs.

WOMAN: He scrapes for breath, gets up; he's running back to her.

MAN: He's reaching.

WOMAN: For what?

MAN: Hands grab hands.

WOMAN: A punch,

MAN: A slap,

WOMAN: A sob,

MAN: A scream,

WOMAN: But who?

MAN: Cloth tears, buttons fall. Then some sharp blow,

WOMAN: Breaking glass/

WOMAN/MAN: Thud.

Darkness swallows them.

WOMAN: Silence.

MAN: Silence. /And he runs.

WOMAN: /And he runs.

MAN: But can't get away.

WOMAN: Surrounded by echoes of laughter songs and fights.

MAN: Songs and fights.

MAN: He packs up boxes, secrets in the night.

WOMAN: Some things left scattered.

MAN: Broken.

WOMAN: Torn. Two chipped tea cups at the sink.

MAN: As the rusty tap drips.

WOMAN: Tomatoes on the vines out back.

MAN: Turned pink at all the things that they've been told.

WOMAN: Grow heavy with rumours.

MAN: Burst red with revelations.

EUGENIA FALLENI enters. She stands silent. Head bowed.

MAN: They find him.

WOMAN: They get her.

MAN: Newspaper headlines:

MAN/WOMAN: The Man-Woman scandal!

WOMAN: The questions, the rumours. The court case.

MAN: The crowd outside the court heaves all breathing
strained – all pushing all waiting to see *It*, to catch its eye.

WOMAN: Women not allowed inside the court make smutty
jokes about the way *it* lied.

MAN: Man on the corner sells drawings of *it* with an evil smile.

WOMAN: First day of the trial, it being led like a dog by the
cops to the court/

MAN: As something red gets thrown/

WOMAN: Something red explodes/

MAN: Hits stains the ladies in the crowd/

WOMAN: And as they scream – *it* looks up at us for just a
moment.

FALLENI lifts her head and looks out.

WOMAN: The truths/

MAN: The lies/

WOMAN: The husbands/

MAN: The wives.

Beat.

MAN/WOMAN: The silence.

*MAN and WOMAN leave FALLENI alone gazing out exposed in stark
white light.*

The lights snap. Black.

OTHER LACHLAN PHILPOTT TITLES

M. Rock
9781783191123

WWW.OBERONBOOKS.COM

Follow us on www.twitter.com/@oberonbooks
& www.facebook.com/oberonbook